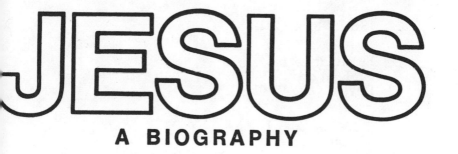

JESUS

A BIOGRAPHY

BY ED LORENZ

LORENZ PRESS

501 EAST THIRD STREET • DAYTON • OHIO • 45401

ISBN: 0-89328-011-9

Lorenz Press, Inc.
501 E. Third St.
Dayton, Ohio 45401

92
Je

18,022

CONTENTS

The Year One 1
The Birth of John the Baptist 5
The Birth of Jesus 11
The Naming of Jesus 17
The Visit of the Wise Men 21
Twelve Years Old 29
Jesus and John the Baptist 37
The Three Temptations 45
The Twelve Apostles 51
The Broken Roof 57
The Temple Pool 63
Jesus Stops a Funeral 69
Stilling the Tempest 73
Jesus and the Crazy Man 79
The Sermon on the Mount 85
The Sermon of the Parables 91
Twelve Baskets of Leftovers 97
The Good Samaritan 103
The Prodigal Son 109
Palms and Psalms 115
Three Days of the Holy Week 121
The Last Supper 127
The Garden of Gethsemane 133
Christ Before Caiaphas 139
Christ Before Pontius Pilate 147
Crucified, Dead and Buried 153
The Empty Tomb 159
Jesus Reappears 165
Visions of Jesus 173

1. THE YEAR ONE

Once upon a time there was a Year One. This was not the beginning of the years or the beginning of the world. The world was already very old; nobody knows quite how old. People had been living on the earth for a long time. They lived in big, mighty nations. They fought many wars in fierce battles. They built large cities. But somehow, everything seemed to start all over again that year, because that was when Jesus came to earth. We have taken it ever since as the most important of all dates. When we say the present year is Nineteen-hundred-and-something, we mean that the Year One was just so many years ago; or Jesus came to earth so many years ago.

One of the interesting things about the Year One is that this was the first year there was what we now call a Christmas Day. Even more interesting is that, although there was a Christmas Day that year, nobody knew it was Christmas and nobody celebrated it. In fact, it was probably some fifty years later that Christmas was recognized, even in the Church, and for many years the evergreen trees grew in the woods and nobody came to get them. Nobody thought of decorating them with lights, or tinsel, or colored glass balls. Nobody sang a Christmas Carol or gave anyone a Christmas present.

Now, in the Year One, there was a country called Judea. This same country is Israel today. In this country there was a quiet, small village hidden among the hills. In this village, called Nazareth, lived a young girl named Mary. I cannot tell you how old she was, but we will guess she was at the age when most young girls of that time got married. Neither can I tell you how she looked or whether her eyes were brown or blue; but we may be sure she had a good and gentle face, and had a calm and pleasing personality.

One day Mary was sitting alone in her room. She may have been sewing, as she was planning to be married, and would be getting ready for the wedding. She was to marry a neighbor, the village carpenter, named Joseph. It was a spring morning; the flowers were in blossom, and the birds were singing. There she sat, with her heart full of beautiful thoughts, when all of a sudden she saw a great, bright light. This light was much brighter than the sunlight streaming through the window. Mary turned to see where this light came from; there, beside the door, dressed all in white, stood an angel. And the angel spoke to her.

Of course, you know that Mary did not speak English. She spoke a language of that day which is similar to the Hebrew now taught in our colleges and seminaries. So we do not know exactly what the angel said to Mary in Hebrew, but it was something like this: "Hello. The Lord God is very pleased with you, and you are to be special among women." And Mary was afraid and began to shake with fear. So the angel said, "Don't be afraid, Mary, for God is very fond of you." Then, while she held her breath and listened, he told her why he was there. God had seen the sin and sorrow that was on the earth, He had heard little children and even grown-up men and women, fathers and mothers, crying because they were so sad. He knew how people were trying to be good and failing at it because they were ignorant or weak. And now God was about to do what He had long promised; He was to come and live among us.

God had lived among men always, just as He does today. He was always everywhere; just as today, we are always in the presence of God. But now He was to make Himself known in a new way. God was going to become a person like us. He was to come, not in royal robes, not as a king to rule, but as a little child, to be born as we are, to grow as we grow. And when God came to earth, Mary was to be His mother.

And Mary replied to the angel, "I am the servant of God. Let him do with me as He wishes." Then the angel left. That was the first day of the Year One.

2. THE BIRTH OF JOHN THE BAPTIST

In the country of Judea the people thought of themselves as members of the tribe of Judah, which was just one of the twelve tribes of Israel. Just as the people in the country of America are called Americans, or the people living in Canada are called Canadians, the people of Judea were called Jews. These Jews believed in God and they had their holy books, or Bible. The Bible they had was what we now call the Old Testament and is part of our Bible today. In these books the coming of God to live on earth was explained; but the explanation was in strange terms or old-fashioned language, so it was somewhat misunderstood by the Jews. They thought that God would come to earth as a king and rule over the whole earth as well as the country of Judea. These books also told of a man who would come ahead of the king to pave the way for His coming.

One day, just before the beginning of the Year One, a strange thing happened to a priest in the Jewish Temple. The priest was a very good old man named Zacharias. He lived with his good wife, Elizabeth, in a quiet little place in the hills, where they were quite respected and loved by all their neighbors. These two old people had wanted to have children, but God had not sent any children to them, in spite of their prayers asking for a little baby. On this day the priest had gone to Jerusalem, the capital of Judea, to take part in the temple services with the other priests, or ministers as we may know them today. These services were going on every day of the year, but there were so many ministers that they had to take turns. Even when a new group came every week, they had to draw straws to see who was to do what duty in the service. In this process Zacharias was chosen to burn the incense. This was the highest of honors for a visiting priest.

Zacharias went in to burn the incense. One part of the Temple was called the *Holy of Holies;* nobody ever went in except the High Priest, and he only once a year. Just outside this *Holy of Holies* was the *Holy Place*. The doors which led to it were covered with gold, and over them hung a heavy curtain of white, blue, scarlet and purple. Inside, there stood a table, and, to the left, a large candlestick with seven branches. Beside the candlestick was an altar for incense, overlaid with gold. Two men went in with Zacharias, one carrying a golden bowl full of incense, and the other a golden bowl full of burning coals. These they put on the altar and went out, leaving Zacharias alone. Outside were many other priests, and many people, all in silence, praying. Zacharias was to take the incense and sprinkle it on the burning coals so as to make a thick fragrant smoke.

This was the time when the strange thing happened. While the old man sprinkled the incense on the coals and the place filled with smoke, suddenly he saw an angel standing beside him. He was afraid. But the angel said to him, "Don't be afraid, Zacharias; your prayer has been heard and your wife, Elizabeth, will have a baby boy. You are to name him John. He will bring you joy and gladness, and many will celebrate the day he is born. He is to be the man to pave the way for the coming of God to live on earth."

Zacharias, from long life and experience, had learned that old people do not have babies. This was the first thought that came into his head. "I am an old man, and my wife is also quite old," he argued. But the angel answered, "You do not know who I am. My name is Gabriel. I come straight from God. He sent me to tell you the great news. But since you do not believe, you will not be able to talk at all until everything I have told you has happened." And he disappeared. Zacharias was struck dumb!

In the meantime, all the people outside were waiting for Zacharias to come out, and wondered why he stayed so long in the *Holy Place*. When he did come out and held up his hands in blessing, he could not talk and could only make signs to them. So he touched his lips and pointed to the sky and they knew he had seen a vision. Then he hastened away to his home to bring his wife the great news. But he had to tell her in signs and in writing, as he could not talk.

After a while Elizabeth did have a baby boy. When he was eight days old, according to the custom in those days, he was named. All the neighbors and relatives were glad that God had heard the prayer of this old couple, so they all came to help in the celebration of his naming day. They all supposed the baby would be named Zacharias, like his father. But Elizabeth said, "No, he shall be named John." They did not know why, so they asked Zacharias. He took a slate and wrote on it, "His name is John." At this very moment he was able to speak again. All the people knew they had seen a miracle and went out wondering what kind of child this was to be. But Zacharias and Elizabeth knew what he would be. They knew the baby, John, would grow up to pave the way for the coming of God to live on earth.

3. THE BIRTH OF JESUS

Months passed after the visits of the two angels. The light green of spring changed into the dark green of summer, and the lillies grew in the fields. The fruits ripened and were picked and brought into the barns for storage. The nights were much colder.

At this time Caesar Augustus, the emperor of Rome, wished to know how many people were living in Judea, so he could make them all pay taxes. Every man had to go to his own city, that is, the place where his family or clan came from. There was a great stir all about the land, with men going to this place or that to have their names written in the census-books. From the little town of Nazareth, Joseph, the carpenter, headed for Bethlehem because he was of the family of David, a former king. With Joseph came Mary, his wife, who was to be the mother of God on earth. Down they came out of the hills like other poor folk, over hills and down valleys, till they arrived in Bethlehem. But when they arrived in town, there was no place for them to stay. Every house was full of guests and the inn was already crowded. The only shelter available was around in back of the inn where they had kept the cows and the donkeys. This was a common stable, with hay all over the floor and dusty cobwebs hanging from the ceilings. There they spent the night. And that night, Mary had her baby, right there in the stable.

Mary, following the custom of the day, carried with her clothes for her baby. This was what we might call a long scarf, or a wide bandage. She used this cloth to wrap around and around her baby boy until he was completely covered. They called these "swaddling clothes." Just as soon as she had covered him with clothes she placed him in a manger, which served as a sort of crib for the night.

Near Bethlehem there were shepherds in a pasture watching over their flocks. We don't see shepherds in this country. A true shepherd never drives sheep. He goes ahead of them and calls them to follow. The sheep, knowing the shepherd's voice, follow him. While the flocks are in the fields, the shepherd stays among them to protect them from wolves and bears.

There are great countries where the grass is green all the year around, and where the only snow is seen on the tops of the mountains. In such countries the sheep can feed in the fields even in the winter.

In the old times, like the Year One, people did not give money each time they went to the synagogue, (or church as we may know it today). Instead, they carried their produce, such as a chicken, a kid goat, or a lamb. That would seem rather odd to you today. Imagine a church where everyone had a lamb, goat or chicken under his or her arm instead of a Bible or prayer book. I am afraid that most small boys and girls would find it hard to sit perfectly still in a church full of frisky little woolly lambs and kid goats. But in the Year One they were used to the custom and did not mind it. People brought them in to give to God. They brought the very best, because they wished to give God the very best they had. Some of these lambs came from the Bethlehem pastures, and the shepherds who took care of the church lambs were gentle and kind men.

On this winter night the stars were shining, and all was still in the fields. The flocks were sleeping while the shepherds watched. We may guess that, while they watched, they talked together and told each other stories. Some stories would be about the former king, David. When he was a boy he had lived in Bethlehem and had spent many a cold night in that very pasture watching his sheep. Once a lion had come after the sheep, and another time a bear, and David fought them and killed them both. The shepherds may have sung the Shepherd's Psalm, "The Lord is my Shepherd." They no doubt spoke to each other about the long-expected ruler that was promised in their Bible, and wondered how he would look and what he would do when he came.

They probably said, "When he comes he will be seen here in Bethlehem," for that was written in their Bible.

As they watched and talked and sang, suddenly something happened.

All at once a very bright light began to shine in the black sky. The night became like day. All the clouds came out in the whites and darks that they have in the early morning and late evening. Out of the center of the shining spot appeared an angel of God, gleaming like a flame of fire. The shepherds got down on their knees and were so afraid they hardly dared to look up. The angel said, "Fear not, for I bring you good news of much happiness and joy to all the people on the earth. For tonight is born a Savior, here in Bethlehem. You can find him, wrapped in swaddling clothes and lying in a manger."

Then the skies grew brighter still, as if the gates of heaven had opened up in the sky. Many angels appeared and sang to the shepherds. This is what they sang:

"Glory to God in the highest,
And on earth peace,
Good will toward men!"

The singing stopped and the angels went back into heaven. The night was dark and still again, and the shepherds were alone. So the shepherds got up and said, "Let's go to Bethlehem and see this Savior!"

Off they went down the road to the stable. There they found Mary and Joseph, and the baby was lying in the manger. They told what they had seen and heard, about the singing angels and the Savior. Mary listened to them, and it reminded her of the things the angel had said to her when he had appeared to her many months ago. The shepherds returned to their fields, praising God for all the wonders of the night.

Carols had been sung by a choir from heaven. God had sent his son as a gift for all the people in the world, to be their Savior.

This was the first Christmas.

4. THE NAMING OF JESUS

A week went by after the night when Mary's baby was born. The day arrived when he was to be given a gift which he could keep for the rest of his life. Many gifts are given to little new babies. Some gifts they play with until they are torn or broken. Others, like spoons or cups, last a long time. But the gift given Mary's baby this day would last always. He would carry it with him wherever he went, even when he became a man. He would never lose it, no matter what happened to him. This gift was his name.

The naming of a child was a matter of such importance that people in those days made a big occasion out of it. It was the custom to pray to God to bless the child, much as we do now at the time of dedication or baptism. The neighbors and family came together, as they did at the naming of little John, the son of Zacharias and Elizabeth, and there was much rejoicing.

It was time to name the baby who had been laid in a manger, though he was no longer in a manger. They had found better lodging for him by this time. Far from home as they were, there would be some neighbors dropping in. The shepherds would be there. It is quite likely that their relatives, Zacharias and Elizabeth, would come with their little boy, John, who was now six months old. There was no question as to the name. Mary and Joseph did not need to decide between this name and that. The angel had told Mary at the beginning what the child would be called, saying, "You will name him Jesus."

Jesus was a very common name. One would think that a name which came straight from heaven, brought by an angel, would be uncommon and beautiful. Or perhaps it would be a new name, that no man had carried since the world began. But the fact is that there were other children by the name of Jesus. It was a plain, ordinary name, like John or James.

This common name of Jesus was the same one that a famous general of that country had had many years before. He had become a national hero, and many boys had been named after him over a period of many years. This general is known to us under the name of Joshua, meaning "the Lord is Salvation." Joshua was the general who led the army of Israel into the promised land. He drove out the people who had been living there, fighting brave battles. Then, like William the Conqueror in England, he settled the country. J-o-s-h-u-a was the

Hebrew spelling. Much later the name of Joshua became J-e-s-u-s, which was the Greek spelling, meaning "Savior."

The Savior had come to earth to be like us and to live the same life we live. He was not given a strange name, or even a royal name, which could make him seem different from us. Joshua was a good man to be named after. The Savior had come to fight hard battles against strong enemies. He had come to save us from our sins. He would lead us into the Kingdom of Heaven.

So the baby Jesus prospered and grew as a child among children, not as a God among Gods.

5. THE VISIT OF THE WISE MEN

The baby Jesus grew and grew, just like any other baby; nothing happened to him except the ordinary things. Then one day a very extraordinary thing happened. Some unusual visitors came to the door of his home.

Nobody knows just exactly how old Jesus was when these visitors came. If you read the account of the visit of the wise men in our Bible, you might think that Jesus was as much as two years old when they came to visit him. If this was the case, it was in Bethlehem that Jesus learned to walk and talk, began to say his prayers, and even learned by heart some of the passages of the Bible.

Far away in the east, during this time, men were watching the sky. Nobody knows exactly where this was. The people of the east lived out-of-doors much more than we do, and the clouds and the stars were of great interest to them. Every night they watched

21

to see the stars rise and set. When a comet blazed across the sky, they would wonder about it. They did not believe the stars were just shining jewels in the night sky. In their imagination they developed a belief that the stars formed mysterious sentences which could be read by anyone who could come to understand the language of the sky. Such translations, they thought, would give them the story of the earth, both past and future. These star gazers were called "wise men." They were well acquainted with the sky, and had names for all the stars they could see.

One night as they looked in the sky, there was a new star which none of them had ever seen before. It seemed to them to shine brighter than all the others, low down in the western sky. They talked about this new star, saying, "There is a new star in the direction of the far away land of the Jews. A king has been born. Let us go and see him."

Off they went on their long journey. Some people believe these men were as great as they were wise; perhaps they were even kings in their own countries. There were three of them: an old man named Casper, a middle-aged man named Melchior, and a young man named Balthaser. There is some speculation that they rode on camels and had a train of servants with them. We can imagine anything we wish about them, because nobody really knows.

On their journey from east to west they finally arrived in the city of Jerusalem. Since they were now in the land of the Jews, it was only natural that they should stop and ask their way. Of course there were no gas stations in Jerusalem in those days, where they could stop to ask directions. Instead, they stopped people on the street to ask, "Where is he that is born king of the Jews? We have seen his star and he is to be a great king, so we have come to pay homage to him."

Well, you can imagine the stir and commotion they caused on the streets of Jerusalem. The people there knew of only one king of the Jews and that was King Herod. He was an old man and did not answer the description of these wise men. They were speaking of a new king, a little child. So the news spread, and as it spread, it was only natural that people would connect it to the promises in their Bible that a king was to come. The people were afraid there might develop a war between the two kings fighting for the crown.

King Herod soon heard of what was happening in the city, and he too was upset. He had heard of the promises in the Jewish Bible that a king would appear to rule the Jews, and he knew that if a new king came, there would be no need for old King Herod. So he decided he had better look into this matter and, if there were any truth to this tale, he should find the new king and kill him while he was still young.

So he called the top priests and lawyers together and asked them: "Your Bible speaks of a new king. Where will he be born when he comes?" The ministers looked in the Bible and there it was, written down in black and white: the new king would be born in Bethlehem. King Herod sent a message to the wise men to meet him in his palace. He asked them many questions. He seemed most anxious to find out just how long ago the star had appeared. Finally, Herod told them to go to Bethlehem, find the child and come back and report to him, so he also could go and pay his respects to the new king. At least that was what he said, but he really meant to go and kill the child.

The wise men left and went to Bethlehem. There they found the child Jesus who had been born on the night the star had appeared. This was easy for them to do, for the star had reappeared and seemed to guide them right to the house where Jesus was living.

The house did not look much like a palace. Joseph was a carpenter, living on his daily wages. He could afford only a humble home. Neither did Jesus look much like a king. He was probably at his mother's knee, looking at the wise men with big eyes, wondering what it was all about. He might even have been more interested in the wise men's camels than in the wise men themselves.

The wise men kneeled before Jesus and paid homage to him. Then they opened their treasures and presented him with gifts of gold, frankincense and myrrh. These were probably kept in odd-looking little boxes and bundles they had brought with them. These gifts were of no use to the child Jesus. Frankincense and myrrh are a kind of fragrant gum resin found on trees and shrubs in the east. We may compare them with the sticky goo we find on pine trees and other evergreens. They were used to make incense that, when put on burning coals, made thick smoke with a sweet smell. Zacharias had placed such incense on the golden altar when he saw the angel. So you see that frankincense and myrrh were used in the worship of God, and the gifts of the wise men were to express the thoughts in their hearts as they spread them out at Jesus' feet. Of course, the gold had great value, but we are not told what happened to it or where it went.

That night both the wise men and Joseph had dreams. In the wise men's dreams God told them about King Herod and warned them not to go back to report to him, but rather to go back to their own countries another way. In Joseph's dream the angel of God appeared and said, "Get up and take young Jesus and his mother and escape into Egypt. Stay there till I send you word to return. Herod will try to find Jesus and kill him." While the wise men were figuring out how to return home by by-passing Jerusalem, Joseph woke up Mary and Jesus and made quick plans for a long journey. Before it was light, they had left Bethlehem by the road to the south.

When daylight came, King Herod woke up and said to himself, "This morning I will know about the new king." The morning passed. The afternoon passed, but no word came from the wise men. At last Herod knew he would hear nothing more from the wise men, and he was very angry. He knew that Bethlehem was the place where the new king had been born, and he also knew, from talking to the wise men, that the new king could not be more than two years old. He sent men from his personal guards to Bethlehem with orders to kill all the little children in the village who were two years old and under. They were too late. Jesus was already on his way to Egypt.

6. TWELVE YEARS OLD

We do not know when, but some time later the family of Joseph, Mary and Jesus came back to Nazareth and settled there. From there, they went on a long journey almost every year. This was done in the early spring, when the leaves were green and the blossoms and wild flowers were pink and white. It was also before the days became too hot, for they lived in a somewhat hot country.

They would start off along the river Jordan, which was east of their home in Nazareth. Here they would pitch their tent and spend the first night. They would turn south the next morning and follow the river for the next two days. This allowed them to miss the country of the Samaritans, because the Samaritans and the Jews were enemies. The third night they would sleep in Jericho. The next morning they would turn to the west, climbing hills along a rough road which was closed in on both sides by high cliffs. On the way they would pass Bethany, which is on the Mount of Olives. A little further on there would be a sudden turn in the road, the walls would open up, and there would be Jerusalem lying down in the valley! It was a beautiful sight. They always looked forward to this first sight of Jerusalem, because this was their destination.

On this annual journey Joseph and Mary were always with lots of other people making the same trip. It would have been dangerous for them to go alone, as there were robbers and hijackers watching this road. So people who went on a trip were careful to travel in a crowd. Joseph and Mary would have many of their friends with them. Half of the people living in Nazareth would be going on the same journey. On the way, other groups would join them from other towns, all bound for the same place, Jerusalem.

Every year in the spring Jerusalem had a big festival called The Feast of the Passover. This festival was a sort of combination of our Easter and our Fourth of July. It was a religious festival, but it was also a celebration of their freedom from slavery in Egypt. In that sense Passover was their national birthday. It came on the fourteenth of Nisan, which was their name for the month. That day and all the week following was a national holiday. Because the festival was held in Jerusalem, the people tried to get to Jerusalem to celebrate it. Many had to stay behind to mind the small children, keep the stores open, tend the sheep and milk the cows, but everyone who was able to manage time off left for Jerusalem.

Until now Jesus had been too young to be taken along on this annual trip. This year he was twelve years old—old enough to go along. Before, Jesus had listened as Joseph and Mary told about their trip after they had come home, and he had wondered just exactly what these sights looked like. Now he too would see the holy city.

They all started out in the beauty of the spring morning, going down along the river and sleeping at night in tents under a full moon. (The Passover was always scheduled to be celebrated during a full moon.) After days of travelling and taking in the many new sights, Jesus found himself looking down on Jerusalem from the Mount of Olives.

Jerusalem was built on hills, and had a thick wall of stone all around it, with a tower at every corner or turn. Crowded inside the walls, white, flat-roofed houses clung to the terraced hillsides. In the middle, and dominating it all, stood a beautiful temple. It was to this temple that Joseph and Mary, holding Jesus by the hand, made their way through the busy streets.

The entry way to the temple was a huge archway leading to a large enclosure or courtyard. This was paved with stone and surrounded by four high walls. Against these walls on all four sides were porches, their roofs held up with stone pillars. This was a crowded area. Not only were there pilgrims like themselves, but there were also people selling doves and lambs to be used as sacrifices during the festival. These were a noisy group; there were even money changers calling out at the top of their voices. In the center stood the Temple itself. A wide stairway with fourteen steps went up to the entrance, which was called the Beautiful Gate. This opened into a large room without any roof called the Court of the Women. Mary waited here, while Joseph and Jesus went up another stone stairway into a room called the Court of Israel. This was separated by a low wall from a third room called the Court of the Priests. Looking over this low wall they could see a large stone altar, and behind that a stone building with a porch and roof. In this building, hidden behind doors and curtains, were two rooms. The first was called the *Holy Place,* and in it stood the golden altar of incense; the other room was the *Holy of Holies,* an empty room whose floor was the jutting rock of the top of the hill.

In the Court of Israel, Joseph and Jesus offered a lamb for their sacrifice. A priest took the lamb and killed it. He cut off a piece of meat, burned it on the fire on the altar, and gave the rest of the lamb back to Joseph. He put the lamb over his shoulder and he and Jesus rejoined Mary in the Court of the Women. From there they left the Temple grounds and went to the home of friends or relatives to prepare the Feast of the Passover.

When evening came they all sat down together and had the roasted lamb for the main course. Along with the lamb they had some bitter herbs, bread and wine. At a prearranged time during the meal, Jesus, as the youngest person in the crowd, had been told to ask, "What does this service mean?" This was the cue for his father to tell the story of the Passover, which went like this:

Long ago the Jews had been slaves in the land of Egypt for several hundred years. The day came when God helped to free them from that slavery. He gave them clear instructions how to go about it. It had to be done in a great hurry, because after many deceitful promises Pharaoh, the ruler of Egypt, had finally allowed them to leave the country. God's instructions to the Jewish people were that each family slaughter a sheep or a goat, and smear some of the blood on the two doorposts of every house in which they would eat their meal. They must eat the roasted meat together with "unleavened" bread which, because of the great haste, was made without yeast. God declared the meal the "Lord's Passover," because in that night He would have the oldest male child of each family in Egypt killed. Those houses which had blood smeared on the doorposts would be "passed over," and the Jews were to leave the following morning.

Pharaoh let the people go, and they began their long, long journey to the Promised Land. God had told them: "You observe this day from generation to generation as a rule for all time, because this was the very day on which I brought you out of Egypt."

When the story was ended, Joseph, Mary, and Jesus, and all their friends sharing the meal sang some songs, the words of which are now in the Book of Psalms in our Bible. The first song was probably the one that started out:

33

"This is the day that the Lord hath made.
We will rejoice and be glad in it."

The following week was set aside for visiting, seeing sights, and going to the services in the Temple. Only too soon came the time to start home again. A lot of other people, thousands of them, were starting out at the same time. With this many people milling around, there was bound to be some confusion. Mary and Joseph went through the main gate, and were back along the Mount of Olives on their way down the Jericho Road, when they missed Jesus. They had noticed that he was not at their side, but had assumed he was with some of the other children sprinkled about in friendly groups. But when he did not show up at supper time, and again not at bedtime, they began to worry. They searched for him in the large crowd traveling with them, but nobody knew where Jesus was; nobody had seen him. At last they realized they must turn back and look for him in Jerusalem. Back in the city they could not find him either—not in the usual places like lodging houses, or the home of friends and relatives.

At last they decided to look in the Temple. There, on one of the many porches, was a crowd of people sitting on the floor listening, while the wise men taught. These teachers were called doctors. They were not doctors of medicine, but doctors of divinity, the teachers of religion. In the midst of the gray-bearded doctors, not only listening, but also asking questions, was Jesus. The people around him were amazed at how well he understood what was being taught, and how eagerly he asked questions to learn more.

You can well imagine how upset Joseph and Mary were by this time. They took Jesus by the hand to take him out of the Temple. Mary said to him, "Jesus, why did you do this to us? You have no idea how we have worried about you and how hard we have hunted for you." And Jesus replied, "Why was it so hard to find me? Didn't you know you would find me in the house of my Heavenly Father?"

Mary was so amazed by this answer that she could not think of anything more to say. So they turned around and left the Temple, and hurried to rejoin their fellow vacationers on the Jericho road.

Back in Nazareth Jesus went back to his normal life. Every day he did just what his parents wanted him to do, learned his lessons, and said his prayers. He learned to help Joseph in the carpentry shop. He grew tall and strong and everybody loved him.

7. JESUS AND JOHN THE BAPTIST

You will remember that, several stories back, we told about the baby John that was born to Zacharias and Elizabeth in their old age. Little John must have stayed at home until he was at least twelve years old. His father and mother would not have allowed him to go off alone until he was at least that old. Of course, his parents may have died while he was just a young child, since they were old when he was born. People in those days did not live as long as they do today.

The next thing, however, we hear about John in the Bible was that he was living in the "wilderness" This means he was not living with other people in a city, town or village. Perhaps he was living out in the woods, or in the desert. He may have gone there because there was no one at home to look after him. But there was a better reason than that. He went into the wilderness because he was told to go there by a voice in his soul. Even as a little boy, he heard this voice calling him and calling him. As he grew older, he was able to understand what it said.

The voice told him that the Christ was coming. This was no secret. Many people knew it and were waiting for the Christ to appear. The voice told John that he was to prepare the way for the Christ. This he had known for a long time. His mother and father had told him many times the story of the angel at the altar, and the message that angel brought from heaven. He knew he was to prepare the way for the Christ by preparing the hearts of men to understand. The voice told him to go into the wilderness. Little by little he came to understand that he was not to be a minister like his father, or a carpenter like his uncle, or a fisherman like his cousin. He was to spend most of his life as a hermit. He was not to live in a house, or walk up and down the streets of towns, but was to be a man of the wilderness, living by himself under the skies and the trees.

No serious work can be done without preparation. A ball game cannot be played without knowing the game and its rules, and practicing it often. The tests in school cannot be passed without studying for them. No one can be a pilot on an airline, or a soldier, or a musician, without preparing for it with study and practice. So it was with John. He had to prepare to be a hermit. He probably spent his vacations studying and practicing to live a life in the wilderness. He had to learn to build a hut, and to make a fire by rubbing two sticks together as the

Boy Scouts do. He had to learn to see a path where there was no path. He had to get acquainted with the habits of the wild bees, so he would know how to gather their honey without getting stung. Someone taught him to make a grasshopper pie, which he would eat instead of meat. He needed to know how to defend himself against the wild animals, so as to live in their natural homeland, the wilderness.

This was only the beginning. His life as a hermit was to prepare him to pave the way for the teachings of the Christ. He had to have a pure heart and had to feel comfortable in the presence of God. What better way to do this than to devote himself completely to God, saying his prayers in the face of the sun, moon, and stars, and feeling and seeing God in the wonderful world about him? This was the way John lived until he was thirty years old.

One day the voice in the soul of John said to him, "Come and stand beside the river. Preach to the people passing by, telling them to wash their sins away in the river in preparation for the coming of Christ. Soon you will find the Christ himself, and you will see the Holy Spirit come down and touch him."

So John went out and stood beside the river Jordan. There was no bridge over it; the road had to cross the river at a shallow spot called a ford. People were coming and going, and they all had to wade across the Jordan at the ford. The wilderness came close to the edge of the river in a tangle of willows and bushes growing among the stones beside the river. John easily stood out among these travelers.

His hair had never been cut, his beard never trimmed or combed. He wore a robe of camel hair, a sort of rough bathrobe, with a leather belt around his middle. Maybe you can picture him in your mind standing there. He was a strong young man with a long staff in his hand. His face and arms were dark brown from the sun and the wind. The piercing look in his eyes was like that of one who had seen God. He was a strong and a striking person, and everyone stopped to see him and listen to him.

There were all kinds of people crossing the river at the ford. Some were going to market with their farm produce. Others were city folks going out to see the farms. There were Roman soldiers, who had conquered the country and ruled it by force. Others came from curiosity because they had heard that a wild man was saying wild things at the ford in the river. There were those who came hoping to find a man of God, and to find a spiritual uplift from his teachings. To all of these various kinds of people John spoke in a loud voice, telling them that the Christ was coming and they should prepare themselves by washing away their sins. Those who repented of their sins he baptized in the river.

All this time Jesus was living in Nazareth. Joseph may have died, because the Bible does not mention him again. With his death Jesus would have become the head of the family. We assume that he worked at the carpenter's shop with saw and hammer, building houses, mending roofs, making doors, tables, and yokes for the oxen. His family grew up around him. He had four brothers, James,

Joses, Jude, and Simon. He also had two sisters. At least two brothers, James and Jude, had got married, so he had little nieces and nephews. When Jesus took these children in his arms, he knew how to hold them. There was always a baby in the carpenter's house.

Nazareth was on a main commercial route, followed by many travelers. It was a rough and tough little town at this time. By growing up there Jesus did not live a sheltered life, in which it was easier to be good than to be bad. He was exposed to continual temptations. He knew all the trials which boys had to meet in public schools and on city streets. He was tempted in all ways just as we are. The difference was that Jesus never sinned. All his life he never did a wrong deed or said an evil word.

One day word came to town that a new preacher—perhaps even a new prophet—was preaching at the ford of the Jordan river. People gathered in the streets after supper to talk about it. Jesus became interested and decided to go hear him for himself.

Eighteen years had passed since he was a boy in the Temple in Jerusalem, listening to the teachings of the doctors. During these years he had come to realize that he was different from other men. As he grew tall and strong, his mind and soul grew and became great. He could feel his strength of spirit as well as his strength of body. As he talked with his brothers in the shop, he knew his thoughts were not their thoughts. He felt that God was near him, so near he could almost touch him with his hand. Like

John the Baptist, he could hear a voice in his soul calling him away from the carpenter's shop and away from Nazareth, to become a leader and a helper of all men. Much of this was dim and vague up to this point. He had not yet come to know himself completely.

When Jesus arrived at the ford of the Jordan he saw John the Baptist in his rough robe and leather belt, preaching to the crowds around him. Sometimes the crowd asked him, "Are you Elijah? Are you the Christ?" And John answered "No." "Who are you then?" they asked. "I am the voice of one preaching in the wilderness. I baptize with water only, teaching people to prepare for the coming of the Christ. The Christ has already come. He stands in the crowd unknown." Then the people asked, "What shall we do?" He told them to repent of their sinful ways.

John spoke very sternly to them against the wickedness in the world. He especially shamed those who pretended to be better than they really were. The people began to respond. One by one at first, and then in ever-larger groups they came up to be baptized, wading out into the river. Jesus also came with a group to be baptized by John. The moment John saw Jesus he realized this was no ordinary person. There was a light in Jesus' eyes that made him different from anyone else. John took a second look and immediately knew that this was the Christ. He said to Jesus, "I must not baptize you. It is for you to baptize me." Jesus insisted, and

42

so John led Jesus into the waters of the Jordan. John baptized Jesus.

Then a wonderful thing happened. The divine voice, which both John and Jesus had been hearing in their souls, now seemed to be speaking to both of them straight from the sky. John saw a dove come down and alight on Jesus. This was the sign which had been promised to him long before, while he was in the wilderness. The voice said, "This is my beloved Son, with whom I am well pleased."

This baptism of Jesus was a very special ceremony. As we know it today, baptism is the ceremony by which persons are admitted to the Christian fellowship of the church, be they child or adult. The baptism of Jesus was more like an "ordination," or the ceremony of entering into the ministry.

8. THE THREE TEMPTATIONS

The baptism by John the Baptist changed the whole life of Jesus. He did not ever go back to the carpenter's shop. The voice from heaven during his baptism made him suddenly realize who he was, and what his mission was. For the first time he knew without any doubt that he really was the Son of God.

It is very hard to say exactly what that means. Even Bible scholars, people who have studied the Bible all their lives, are not able to make us understand it completely. Some things, however, are quite plain.

It is plain that Jesus was the Christ. Christ is a Greek name, just as Messiah is a Hebrew name. Both mean the same thing—one who is anointed. It was by anointing, that is, by pouring fragrant oil on one's head, that a person was made a priest, a king, or a queen. Saying that Jesus was the Christ is the same as saying that this man was called into God's service, and that he received his wisdom and his strength from God. The people of that country had been looking for an Anointed One who would be both their king and their high priest. As a king he was to make them great, and as a priest he was to make them good. Vague, mysterious things were said about him in their Bible. They were expecting him, but in a temple or in a palace, not in a carpenter's shop. When the spirit of God came down from heaven, as a dove, during his baptism, God anointed Jesus. He is the Christ. God is in Jesus, and through him God tells us of His love and of His will.

Jesus immediately went away alone, looking for a place where he could think this all out. He went into the same wilderness that John had just left. There he spent many days in silence, thinking and thinking. He was planning his new life, and considering what it was to mean for him and for the world. Later he told his disciples about this time in his life. He said, "The devil came and spoke to me," meaning that one wrong thought after another came into his mind to bother him.

Jesus went on telling about a day during that time when he was very hungry. He had thought for so long and so hard that he had forgotten about food. At last he noticed a visitor standing next to him. When he looked up to see who it was, he knew it was the devil. The devil began in a very friendly way, as he always does, "It is a long time since you have eaten anything. You must be very hungry. If you are the Son of God, speak to those flat stones and turn them into bread. The Son of God can do that. Pretty soon you will be going out into the world to tell people about God. You will not be a carpenter any more. How will you get anything to eat? Make your own bread. Use your divine powers to help yourself." In this way the devil tried to get Jesus to think of himself and his comforts first, and to worry about his mission in life later. But Jesus had turned his back on that kind of life. He said to the devil, "It is written in the Bible that man shall not live by bread alone, but also by every word that comes out of the mouth of God." That was the first temptation.

The devil pretended to agree with Jesus, and answered, "Of course the body is not nearly as important as the soul. It is best to do the will of God even if we go hungry. We ought to think only of God and not of ourselves. Come with me and we will show our faith." The devil led Jesus to the holy city of Jerusalem. There they stood on top of one of the high towers of the Temple. They looked down, and the people on the ground below looked like ants crawling around. "Now," said the devil, "let us rely on the word of God. God says His angels will protect all those who love Him. Why don't you jump off this tower?" This was a great temptation. Jesus knew that God would not let him fall and be killed. If he jumped, he could show the crowd the wonderful power of God; by seeing such a spectacular deed the people would believe that Jesus truly was the Son of God.

Many people have met the first temptation of bodily comfort and have overcome that tempting;

47

some have been tempted to neglect or abuse their bodies; others even think God will be pleased if they do not eat, or if they whip themselves, or break the laws of nature. These are also temptations of the devil.

Jesus replied to the devil, "It is written in the Bible,'Thou shalt not tempt the Lord thy God.' " That means we are not to risk our lives to see if God will save us. We are to be careful not to pay too much attention to our bodies, but we must also not neglect them. This was the second temptation.

These two temptations, you see, are like the rocks on both sides of a narrow river. Some people, trying to swim down the river of life, have hit the rocks on one side, crawled ashore, and lived the lives of worldly comfort. Others have struck the rocks on the other side, and have become fanatics, doing foolish and crazy things. Jesus did neither. Avoiding the rocks on either side is what people mean when they say you should "walk the straight and narrow."

The devil was very patient and was not discouraged. He said to Jesus, "I know what you want. You want the whole world to be good and happy. Let's go up on this high mountain where we can see the world." Up the mountain they went. There the whole world was spread out at their feet like a great map. It was a sight Jesus had seen many times from a hill near Nazareth. Jesus looked, with a great desire in his heart to help men and women, and to save them. In all the towns below, sin and sorrow lived among the people because the devil had them in his power. The devil said, "All this I will give you; I will leave the world in peace. I will go out of the lives of the people and joy will come into all their lives, if you will do one thing. Here, in this lonely place, where no one can see us, kneel down before me and worship me!"

It was as if the devil had said to Jesus, "You cannot govern the world without me. You cannot even begin your great plans without my help. If you decide to always do the right thing, to be perfectly good and have only the highest ideals, you will fail. That is the truth. You will get yourself killed." Jesus answered him by saying, "Get behind me, Satan. It is written in the Bible, 'Thou shalt worship the Lord thy God, and Him only shalt thou serve'."

The devil left Jesus. He had been beaten. The Lord God sent angels to Jesus to minister to his needs.

9. THE TWELVE APOSTLES

Jesus came back out of the wilderness after about a month there. He still had on his carpenter's clothes, so people did not know who he was. With most people, clothes mean a lot. He came out of the wilderness at the same spot where he had entered it, right there by the ford in the Jordan river. John the Baptist was still there, preaching and baptizing. As Jesus came slowly down the road, John looked over the heads of the crowd and saw him. He turned to two men listening to him and said, "There he is now. There is the Christ." Immediately the two men followed Jesus.

One of these men was named Andrew, and the other was named John. We will call him John the Apostle, to keep him separate from John the Baptist, although after this we will not hear much about John the Baptist again. Andrew and the new John were fishermen on the Lake of Galilee. They lived in Capernaum and were partners in the fishing business. Both of them had brothers. Andrew's brother was named Peter, and John's brother was named James. They were all partners together, these four friends.

Each of these sets of brothers had good mothers. The mother of Andrew and Peter was named Mary, and the mother of John and James was named Salome. These mothers were neighbors and very good friends. Both of them also became friends of Jesus and his followers, and went about with them, caring for them. Salome had been a friend of Jesus since his boyhood, because she was his aunt. Jesus' mother, Mary, was her sister. So you can see that James and John were the cousins of Jesus. It is quite likely they all grew up together, and Jesus had known all four of these fishermen for many years. Capernaum is only a short distance from Nazareth.

Andrew and John were the first to join Jesus after hearing what John the Baptist said about him. Jesus heard their footsteps as they came hurrying after him, and turning around, he said, "Whom are you looking for?" They bowed to Jesus and said, "Master, where are you staying?" Jesus replied, "Come and see." So all three went on together and spent the rest of the day talking among themselves, asking questions and answering them.

The next day Andrew found Peter, and John found James. Both of them brought their brothers to Jesus. Then Jesus himself found Philip, who was already a friend of the four partners, and was also a fisherman. Philip had a friend named Bartholomew who lived in Cana, not far from Nazareth. Philip told Bartholomew that they had found the Christ, that his name was Jesus, and that he had come from Nazareth. Bartholomew could hardly believe it. He knew Nazareth as a homely little town. It seemed impossible that any good thing could come out of Nazareth. Philip said, "Come and see." Bartholomew came, and he believed.

In this way six friends gathered around Jesus. As fishermen, these men had lived healthy and happy lives filled with patience and courage. They had lived out of doors with the wind and the rain in their faces. They were used to sudden storms, so they knew how to live with danger. As friends they had not only fished together, but also talked together. No doubt they had talked about the sermons in their church, and the world in which they lived. They were manly, open-minded men—just what Jesus needed as followers.

Some months later Jesus invited six other men to join his followers. One was named James, and was called "Little James" to keep him separate from Jesus' cousin. He may have been shorter, but we do not know. Another was named Thomas, a very matter-of-fact person inclined to look on the gloomy side of things. Two men were named Judas; to tell them apart, one added "Iscariot" to his name. Still another was named Simon, who belonged to a wild secret society called the Zealots. They were constantly laying plans against the Romans. The last man to be asked was Matthew. There is a little story about his being called.

There was a highway running through Capernaum, somewhat like our interstate highways. Sometimes it was called the Way of the Sea, but more often it was called the Great Western Road. It connected the lands of the east with the lands of the west, and extended from Damascus to the coast of the Mediterranean Sea. Caravans, like convoys of trucks, were constantly going over it, delivering goods from the east to the west, and from the west to the east. The Romans had paved it and kept it in good order and repair. For this service they collected a toll. There was a toll gate at Capernaum, and one of the men who sat at the gate was Matthew. Many people disliked Matthew because he worked for the Romans. The Romans were their conquerors, and people felt that good Jews should not work for their masters. Few respectable people had anything to do with him. He had money and a large house, but the only people who made friends with him were those who also worked for the Romans. He had even been banished from the church.

Matthew was a good man in spite of being a tax collector. The other followers knew all about him. They had also learned that Jesus did not care about the popularity of any man. Wherever he found a good man he loved him. Jesus was speaking to the people almost every day near the toll gate. Every word he spoke was heard by Matthew, went into his heart, and stayed there. One day after the sermon,

Jesus walked past the gate, held up his hand to Matthew, and said, "Follow me." Matthew did not hesitate a moment, but stood up, left his job, and followed him. It must have been very hard for Simon to accept Matthew, whom he and all his other secret society friends had hated so much.

That night Matthew gave a big dinner party at his house for all his friends. Matthew felt just as Andrew and John had felt. He had learned to know and love Jesus, and wanted all his friends to know him also.

It was in this way that the twelve apostles were gathered together. The Twelve were to represent the twelve tribes of Israel. They were sometimes called disciples, which means "pupils," but they were also called apostles, which means "men who are sent."

10. THE BROKEN ROOF

The first part of the ministry of Jesus was spent around the Lake of Galilee.

Even though he went from town to town, he still could look back from the tops of the hills and see the shining blue waters of the lake. With him went his friends, or apostles, who were now sharing his life with him. This made for pleasant company, walking along the green valleys talking together. Then at noon they would gather in the shade of trees and talk some more.

Jesus would preach in the market places of the little towns. There always seemed to be a crowd of people gathered in these towns to hear him tell them about the kingdom of heaven. If they wished to see it, they should confess their sins. Those who would see it, would find it beautiful and satisfying beyond their greatest imagination. This came to be called the gospel, which means the good news. (So you see, when you hear of anyone preaching the gospel, it means the good news.)

In all of these small towns and large towns he found sick people. Part of his mission was to touch them with his hands and make them well. This he tried to do quietly and privately, because he did not like to have large crowds excited or staring at him. Sometimes he asked the sick not to tell anyone who had healed them, but of course they were so happy and thankful they could not keep it a secret from their friends. This caused the crowds to become larger, and the best thing for him to do was to go into the country. There the crowds could gather more closely around him and hear him better.

One day he went back to Capernaum and went into a house, probably Peter's house. The people heard he was there, and the street in front of the house became quite congested. There was a young man in Capernaum who was paralyzed so badly that he could not walk. He had nothing to look forward to in his life except pain and uselessness to others. You can imagine his thoughts as he lay on his bed all day long, with nothing to do—having to ask someone to do things for him, never being able to pay them back in any way. Finally he realized he was sick in his soul as well as in his body. He knew he had sinned in his thoughts, and it was much worse to have a sick soul than a sick body. But he was sick in both body and soul. This young man had four friends. These four heard that Jesus was in town and decided that their young sick friend should go to Jesus to be healed of his paralysis.

The sick man was on a very simple kind of bed. It was really just a blanket spread out on the floor. The four friends came in, and each picked up a corner of the blanket; together they carried him down the street. When they came near Peter's house they saw the crowd. It was so large that they were certain they could not get through it. They knew Jesus was in the house, but they could not get to him. What should they do?

The house, like all the other houses in the village, was only one story high and had a flat roof. The roof was used in the early morning and early evening to sit on and enjoy the cool breeze. There was a stairway up to the roof from the outside. The four men decided to go to the roof. Up they went, with the front two men stooping low and the back two men raising their hands well over their heads in order to prevent their sick friend from falling out of the blanket. When they got to the top, they found an opening in the roof and enlarged it even further. When it was large enough, they lowered the bed-blanket through the opening with their ropes, until he lay right at the feet of Jesus.

Jesus looked up at the four men, and then looked down at the sick man. He was so glad to see how sure they were that he could heal their friend. The sick man's face was like an open book to him. His eyes pleaded, "Please help me. Help me get rid of my sickness and my sins." Jesus said to him, "Your sins are forgiven." Jesus knew that to have a sick soul was worse than any sickness of the body, so he cured his soul first.

In the crowd around Peter's house were a number of scribes. These were educated men connected with the church, who would study the Bible, and would also write about it. Now, you know that their Bible, our Old Testament today, is a collection of many sacred old books; the scribes wanted no changes in it. Anything new that came along they did not want. They had become distrustful of Jesus, because he was preaching new ideas that they could not find in their readings and writings. When these scribes heard Jesus say, "Your sins are forgiven", they were shocked. They began to whisper together behind their hands, saying, "How can this man forgive sins? Only God can forgive our sins." Jesus could read their minds, just as well as he had read the eyes of the sick man. So he said to the scribes, "Why do you wonder so about what I have said? Which is easier to say, 'Your sins are forgiven,' or to say, 'Rise up and walk?' So that you will know the Son of man has power on earth to forgive sins, I tell you," and he turned to the sick man saying, "Get up and walk. Roll up your bed and go to your own house." Immediately the young man got up from his blanket, picked it up, and walked out of Peter's house. All the crowd was amazed and talked together about the strange thing they had seen and heard. But the scribes were speechless.

Jesus told his disciples later that they were to do the same kind of things as he had done that day. Any time they found a sinner who was sorry for his sins, they were to tell him of the forgiveness of God. The scribes, however, searched in their old books. They found that the priests in the Temple could forgive sins, but they found nothing to justify these words of Jesus. In this way the deed of mercy Jesus did that day only made the scribes more bitter toward him. It was at this time they started thinking of ways to get rid of Jesus.

11. THE TEMPLE POOL

One day Jesus and his disciples decided to go to Jerusalem for the celebration of one of their festival days. In past stories I have described to you the Temple in Jerusalem, but I did not tell you about the pool just outside this Temple.

This pool was fed by a spring that came up out of the ground. Usually the pool was calm and glassy, but every once in a while it became agitated on the surface. Nobody could figure out just why it did this. In those days, when something like this could not be explained, they would say it was caused by spirits, either good or bad. If they were good spirits, they called them "angels." The story had spread around Jerusalem that an angel would come down to this pool once in a while and stir up the water. After the water had been touched by an angel, they believed it became holy water; the first person to get into the pool after the stirring up would be healed of any disease he or she had. This pool had become so famous as a healing spot that there were lots of sick people constantly close to its banks; from there they could see the water stirred up and would try to be the first to get into the pool. Some people had friends with them to help them into the water quickly when the time came.

There was one man who had been ill for a long, long time—thirty-eight years to be exact! He had been at the pool for some time, but was not ever able to be the first in the water. As Jesus came to the Temple in Jerusalem he passed by the pool. When he saw this man, he knew of his dilemma just by looking at him. Jesus felt sorry for the man and said to him, "Do you want to get well?" To get well! Yes, that was what this man had wished for all these years. He had almost given up hope. He said to Jesus, "I am only a poor man and I have no friends to help me get into the pool after it had stirred. Someone always beats me to it." Then Jesus said to him, "Get up. Pick up your bed and walk."

The man immediately started to get up. That showed he had a lot of faith in Jesus. He probably had never seen him before, and might not even have heard of him. But now he saw him, heard his voice, and believed in him with all his heart. Some men might have said, "I can't do that. I am a sick man, and I haven't been able to walk for thirty-eight years." This man believed and tried to get up. God gave him the strength to stand. He picked up his bed and walked away.

It just so happened that this day was the Sabbath day for the Jews. Their Bible was full of rules and laws, and they tried to follow these rules and laws to the extent that it sometimes became ridiculous. One commandment, for instance, said there should be no work on the Sabbath. They had carried that thought to the point, where even to carry anything on the Sabbath was considered work. Their ministers had been so anxious for the Sabbath to be a day of rest that they tried to keep people from doing anything at all. When this man, with his glad face, was jumping up and down, first on one leg and then on the other, to make sure they both were strong and able, they noticed he was carrying his bed wrapped up in his arms. They stopped him and said, "This is the Sabbath day. It is not lawful for you to carry your bed around." He replied, "I have been sick. I have been lying on this bed for thirty-eight years. The man who cured me told me to pick up my bed and walk." Then they asked him in an angry voice, "Who is this man that told you that?" They did not think it was such a good and wonderful thing that this man had been cured from his sickness. All they thought about was that one of their little rules had been broken. They were angry with the man for having been healed, and with the man who had healed him. It seems wrong to us that these scribes should think more of their rules than of man's bodily or spiritual welfare. This kind of people made many complaints about Jesus all during his ministry, because he went right on doing good deeds, no matter what day of the week it was.

Fortunately, this time, the healed man did not know the name of the man who had cured him, so he could not answer their question; and Jesus, meanwhile, had gone away into the crowd. Some time later Jesus found the man again and told him, "You have been healed. Try not to sin any more, because if you do, an even worse thing will happen to you." By this he meant that sin is worse than sickness, and disease of the soul is worse than disease of the body.

12. JESUS STOPS A FUNERAL

You remember I told you that Nazareth was in the hills looking over a great plain. From Nazareth you could look across the plain and see the white buildings of a little town called Nain, built on another hillside. The word "nain" means "pleasant," and pleasant it was. It was situated among trees and looked out east, north, and west at the high mountains, and it even had a glimpse of the blue sea when the air was clear and the sun was shining. In this village there was a poor widow with her son. He was her only support, and without him she would not be able to buy food and clothing. One day this son became sick, and finally he died. It was very sad; everyone in the village felt sorry for the poor widow, and all came out to the funeral and cried with her over the loss of her son.

A rough, steep path led from Nain. Down this path came the funeral procession. First the women, all crying and praying out loud for the widow. Then came young men carrying a wide flat board which held the body of the dead son. Then came the mother, and after her the rest of the townspeople. As they all started down the path, another group started up. This was an entirely different kind of crowd, made up of the countryfolk round about. Some were fishermen, some farmers in rough clothes. Among them was one man dressed like them who seemed to stand out in the crowd. As they started up the path, he would talk, and all the rest would listen with reverence and eagerness. About half way up the hill the two groups met. Jesus saw the poor mother and was very sorry for her. He immediately said to her, "Don't cry;" he reached out and touched the board on which the dead son lay. The young men who carried the board stopped, and the mother also stopped to see what was going on. The people from both groups gathered around. Jesus said, "Young man, I want you to get up," and the dead man came to life and began to talk to his mother. Finally, he sat up, got off the board, and walked down the path with his mother and Jesus. So the funeral procession turned around and started back up to Nain. The women who had been crying wiped their eyes, and all the people praised God for this miracle. Some of them said, "A great prophet has grown up among us," others, "God has visited his people today."

This story shows that Jesus cared about the sorrows of people. Sometimes death comes into families in such a way that it seems God does not care. It is then we should remember that day in Nain. God does not always stop a funeral, but he does care. He has pity for those in sorrow. We also know that God raises us from our deepest sleep to the light of each new day. Every morning he gives us back our life.

13. STILLING THE TEMPEST

Once, Jesus had been preaching off and on all day, and he was very tired. He wanted to be able to stop and rest, but the people would not leave him alone. They begged him to continue teaching and preaching, and he knew that they would follow him anywhere he went. He had learned by now that the best way to handle this kind of problem was to have the crowd gather on the shore of the Lake of Galilee, while he preached to them from a boat just off the shore. On this day Jesus motioned to John and Peter, and they pulled up the anchor and rowed the boat out away from the shore and the crowd. Some of the people ran down to the shore and took all the available boats to row after them, so that they could continue to hear the great words that Jesus was preaching. But all of them failed to look up at the sky and see that a great storm was brewing. When the winds came, they were taken by surprise.

You might think that everyone liked what Jesus had to say. Really, this was not true. Some of them did not like what he did on the Sabbath, as we saw in the past few stories; others did not like to hear him speaking for God, as we also have seen. These were his enemies, and they were growing in numbers. Jesus could see their faces as he spoke to them, and he knew they objected to what he was saying. This made it very hard for him to continue to preach.

On this day, after all that hard work, the first thing Jesus did after the boat pulled away from shore was to go to the back of the boat, lie down and go to sleep. It was after he went to sleep that the winds started to blow with more and more force, until there was a full storm roaring. Great big black clouds came out from behind the hills. The white-capped waves grew in size and began to slop over the side of the boat. The bottom of the boat soon was full of water, and some of the fishermen had to stop rowing and begin to bail out the boat. The wind continued to blow harder and harder; the waves grew higher and higher, while roaring louder and louder, and the boat rocked more and more. At last the fishermen became frightened for their safety. The water was coming in faster than they could bail.

This was an unusual situation. These fishermen had grown up on the lake. Ever since childhood they had seen storms on the lake and were used to having to seek safety before it became too rough. But this time the storm caught them by surprise, and they felt the storm had gone beyond the ability of their boat to carry them with safety. What to do? These experienced fishermen did a strange thing. They woke up Jesus, who they thought was a carpenter who knew little or nothing about boats, and asked him to save them from the storm. They shook him and said, "Master, we are sinking and we will all die. Do something!" Now, what good can a carpenter do for a boat in the water that is about to sink in a bad storm? Remember, Jesus came from a town in the hills where the only water he saw was at the bottom of a well. These fishermen knew that. This makes it even more unusual that they should ask him for help. We must assume from this that they were very aware that Jesus could perform miracles. They knew that he was the wisest, strongest, and best man they had ever known. They knew that only God could save them and their boat from destruction, and that Jesus could call on God for help. So they woke Jesus up from his sound sleep and said, "Master, we are sinking and we will all die. Do something!"

Jesus got up and raised his hands over the water and said, "Peace, be still." Suddenly the wind stopped blowing and the waves calmed down, and all was peaceful. Jesus then turned to the fishermen and said, "Why are you so afraid? Don't you have any faith in me?" Now they were almost as afraid of Jesus as they had been of the wind and the waves. They turned to each other and, behind their hands, said to one another, "What kind of man is our friend

Jesus, that he can tell even the wind and the waves to stop, and they obey him?"

Later, when the disciples told this story to others, they also liked to tell the story about the time they were out on the lake alone, and the wind and the waves had built up to a furious pitch. That time they saw some movement off to one side, and there in the middle of the lake was a figure, walking on top of the water. As it approached, they thought it was a ghost. It turned out to be Jesus, coming out to help them. He walked across the waves as if he were on a grassy field. He got into the boat and the wind stopped blowing; the waves calmed down, and they could row to shore without danger.

These stories have never been explained. If the winds of disaster blow upon us, and the waves of misfortune rise and rock our boat, Jesus may seem to us to be far distant or asleep, or on shore. Then when he comes to our help across the rough water, it seems too good to be true; we cannot believe our eyes, and we are tempted to think it must be just plain luck that saved us from the storm.

This much is plain: if we have Jesus in our hearts, no storm of life will ever make us sink.

14. JESUS AND THE CRAZY MAN

After the calming of the storm by Jesus, the boat in which he and his fishermen friends were riding crossed the lake and landed on the other side. The people who lived there were all heathen. They were Greeks, probably descendants of the soldiers of Alexander the Great who had conquered this part of the world. Now that the Romans were the masters by force of arms, these Greeks lived in a place by the lake that was steep and rocky, with rivers running down from the countryside. As Jesus and his disciples came near the shore, they saw a strange sight. On their side of the lake such a sight could never have been seen. The Jews did not eat pork at all, and most Jews even today still do not eat pork. They would never think of having a herd of pigs. But the Greeks ate pork, and they also supplied it to the Roman soldiers in that area.

The Jews were not only particular about eating and even touching pork, but they also had superstitions about touching anything that was dead. They thought that pigs were unclean, that anything dead was unclean, and any one not Jewish was unclean. If they touched "unclean" things, they had to go through a religious ceremony: they had to wash themselves, while praying the right prayers, in order to cleanse themselves and make themselves pleasing to the sight of God. The enemies of Jesus had heard how he had raised people from the dead, and they did not like it, because he had touched something unclean. The fact that he had performed a miracle did not enter their minds. All they could think of was the fact that he had disobeyed their laws about cleanliness.

Now, as the boat approached the shore the sight they saw was this: up on the cliffs overlooking the lake was a herd of pigs being tended by Greeks, who were also considered unclean, and to top it all off, there was a graveyard alongside the field of pigs. So here were three unclean things at the same time.

To make matters worse, down the hill beside the cliffs a wild man came running. We nowadays think of such a man as crazy. He had been living in the caves and holes in the graveyard along with the dried bones of the dead people, so he was about as unclean as anyone could be. At night, those passing the area could hear him crying and screaming in a loud voice. In the daytime most people would keep their distance from him, but they would see him running about, wringing his hands and cutting himself with sharp stones, so he was always covered with dried blood. The man did have a home, and a few friends. Sometimes they would come, catch him, and tie him up to try to keep him from cutting himself so badly. The man was like Samson; he would break those ropes, and even chains.

This did not seem like a very good place to land the boat. Probably, if the fishermen had been without Jesus, they would have pushed out again and found a place with better surroundings. As it was, they probably hung back and let Jesus go ahead of them to see how he got along there, before they ventured very far ashore. The crazy man did not try to hurt anyone. He came close to Jesus, got down on his knees in front of him, and yelled, "You are the Son of the Most High God. What have I to do with you?" You see, the crazy man had an evil spirit and he talked through his voice. Jesus then commanded the evil spirit to leave the man. He replied, "Don't torment me." Jesus asked, "What is your name?" and the spirit answered, "Legion."

Now, the word "legion" means a large number of Roman soldiers, but when the spirit said its name was Legion, it meant that there were many evil spirits living in this crazy man.

"Do not torment us," pleaded the spirits, "if you drive us out, send us into that herd of pigs." "Begone!" Jesus said. Suddenly the pigs grunted wildly and raced toward the steep cliffs. The men in charge had lost all control over them. The whole herd rushed over the edge of the cliffs into the lake below, and perished in the water.

The pig-keepers were stunned for a moment. Then they turned around and ran into the little town, telling everyone there that a thousand devils had gone out of the crazy man and into the pigs. So the owner came to see what had happened. There were the pigs, drowned in the lake, and there was the man sitting calmly at the feet of Jesus, fully clothed and in his right mind. When the disciples told the owner what had happened, he was both afraid and very angry. He was much more concerned about his pigs than he was about the man who had been crazy. So he turned around and ordered Jesus off his land. He told him that he was not welcome in that area at all.

The man who had been crazy asked Jesus if he could follow him and become one of his disciples. But Jesus told him that the best thing he could do was to go back home, join his wife and children, and tell all his neighbors what great things God had done for him. Jesus and the others went back into the boat and rowed away over the dark lake. The healed man went into the town and stopped all he met, telling them of the power and the love of Jesus.

I wonder—if you owned some pigs, or a store, or a house, or even some money, and God used it all to help another man in trouble—what would you think? Would you drive God out of your town, or maybe, out of your heart?

15. THE SERMON ON THE MOUNT

People came from all around to see and hear Jesus. Some came because they hoped they would see with their own eyes one of the miracles they had heard Jesus could perform on the sick. Some were there because they themselves were sick and wanted to be healed by him. Others came because they were poor, hungry, or disliked by their neighbors, and wanted to know what Jesus had to say about making the world a better place to live in. Very few of the important people came. The rich, those in high government places, and the ministers, all stayed away. The people who were most often seen in church, and made a show of their prayers and Bible reading (so they would be thought of as being good), disliked Jesus very much. The priests and the ministers criticized him and objected to what he said and did. The people surrounding Jesus did not look like the same congregation that was seen in the synagogue on the Sabbath day.

There were often large crowds following Jesus. He did not usually preach long sermons. He liked best to speak to a few people in a quiet and friendly way, while walking in the country or sitting under a tree, or in a boat. Twice, however, he preached to a large crowd at great length. Once, he was sitting in a boat offshore, teaching the crowd on land in many parables, which are stories. The other time it happened on a mountain, where he preached the "Sermon on the Mount," as we have come to call it. He began this sermon by preaching eight beatitudes. We call it so, because the word "beatitude" means happiness and blessedness, and that's what Jesus talked about.

Nobody knows where Jesus preached the Sermon on the Mount. All the hills around the Lake of Galilee look much alike, and all are different from Mount Sinai. The eight beatitudes were told to a large crowd on a gentle hill overlooking the lake, with green grass and shrubs all the way to the top. We may guess that the sun was shining, the birds were singing, and the flowers were sprinkled throughout the grass, because Jesus mentioned the flowers and the birds; he told how God takes care of them every day. The people sat on the grass just downhill from Jesus, who sat at the foot of a big tree. He spoke to the poor, the sad, the sinful, and the outcast; he told them eight ways to be happy. This is what he said:

"Blessed are the poor in spirit;
    for theirs is the kingdom of heaven.

"Blessed are they that mourn;
    for they shall be comforted.
"Blessed are the meek;
    for they shall inherit the earth.
"Blessed are they which hunger and thirst
    after righteousness;
    for they shall be filled.
"Blessed are the merciful;
    for they shall obtain mercy.
"Blessed are the pure in heart;
    for they shall see God.
"Blessed are the peacemakers;
    for they shall be called the children of God.
"Blessed are they which are persecuted for
    righteousness' sake;
    for theirs is the Kingdom of Heaven."

What does this all mean? The true source of happiness is in our hearts. Happiness does not come from the house in which we live, or the clothes we wear, or the money we have. Happiness is within ourselves. If we try to do right so that God will approve of us, we will be happy, no matter what things happen to us. There is a great difference between happiness and wealth, but happiness and goodness always will be found together.

Later, in the same sermon, Jesus told the crowd that the Ten Commandments are to be kept with our hearts, as well as with our hands and mouths. He showed that the commandment "Thou shall not kill" really forbids us even to think hateful thoughts about our friends or neighbors.

Then he taught the people how to pray, and said: "This is how you should pray:

> "Our Father which art in heaven,
> Hallowed be thy name,
> thy kingdom come,
> thy will be done,
> in earth, as it is in heaven.
> Give us this day our daily bread.
> And forgive us our debts,
> as we forgive our debtors;
> And lead us not into temptation,
> but deliver us from evil:
> For thine is the kingdom, and the power,
> and the glory, for ever. Amen."

It is our "Lord's Prayer," and the words may be very much like those you say. Jesus shows us that if we wish to be happy, we must do things that are right and good, and we must ask God every day to help us and bless us. Prayer is as necessary to the life of our soul as food is to the life of our body.

Then Jesus gave the Golden Rule: "Do unto others as you would have them do unto you." Later, he put it in another and still stronger way: "A new commandment I give unto you, that you love one another; as I have loved you, that you also love one another." He said that we ought to love even those who hate us, trying to do them good in return for the evil which they do to us. He said, "It is easy to love your friends, but my true followers will love their enemies."

At the end of his sermon he compared the crowd to two houses. "Once," he said, "there was a wise man who built his house upon a rock. Down he dug into the earth until he found solid rock, and there he set the foundation for his house. Then a storm came, the rains fell, and floods followed. The winds came and hit against that house, but it did not fall, because it was based on a solid rock. That house," he said, "is like the people who hear my teachings, listen to them with attention, and then do what I have said.

"Every one that hears these sayings and does not do them is like the foolish man," Jesus continued, "who built his house upon the sand. The rains came and the floods followed. The winds blew and hit against the house. That house completely collapsed.

16. THE SERMON OF THE PARABLES

Jesus did not preach this sermon on a mountain, but rather on a lake. He sat in a boat offshore while he was speaking, and the people sat or stood on the bank. The sermon was all in stories. Most of them were quite short, but one was rather long. These stories are called "parables," which means they were not told just for the sake of telling a story, but rather to teach a truth by putting it in story form to make it more understandable.

All these parables were about the kingdom of heaven. Because of the promises in their Bible, the people were looking and praying for the coming of the kingdom of heaven. They were expecting a king who would sit on a throne. They wanted such a king to conquer their enemies, and again make them a free and rich nation. In these stories Jesus tried to show the people the true idea of the kingdom of heaven. This kingdom, he said, is not like the kingdoms of the world. It is not on the map, but in the heart. Its power is truth. Those who belong to it should try to live, here on earth, the life of heaven, which is the life of goodness and usefulness, with love for man and God.

Jesus said that the kingdom of heaven is like a beautiful pearl. For one rare and beautiful pearl a man sold everything he had and bought it. That's how it is with the kingdom of God. The joy of knowing God and keeping his commandments fills our hearts with such great happiness that nothing else matters.

Then he said that the kingdom of heaven is like yeast. It is mixed in with the dough; the dough rises, and eventually becomes bread. This means that the citizens of the kingdom of heaven little by little change the world in which they live, making it as different from the present world as bread is from dough.

Again, Jesus said that the kingdom of heaven is like a grain of mustard seed. It is one of the smallest seeds known, but it grows into a large plant. You can see that by this Jesus meant the kingdom of heaven had a very small beginning. It had only a handful of disciples, but the kingdom would grow and grow until it included the whole world.

These were the short parables. The long story was the story of the sower.

Once upon a time a man went out to sow seeds in his field. The man had a large bag of grain hanging from his belt. As he walked, he put his hand into the bag, bringing out a handful of grain and scattering it over the ground. In the middle of the field there was a path. It was walked on all day and had become packed down and hard from use. Some of the seed fell on this hard path. There was a place on one side where the soil was very thin over a large rock just under the surface. Some of the grain fell on this soil. In a corner of the field was a patch that had been full of briars and thorns the year before, and these were just getting ready to sprout again this year. Some of the grain fell on this spot. The rest of the field was good ploughed land, ready for seed. The rest of the grain fell on it.

The man with the bag went back and forth, scattering the grain in the field. Pretty soon a man came along the path wearing heavy boots. He stepped on some of the seeds and ground them into small pieces. Not long after that a small bird saw the pieces on the path, came down and ate a bit, then flew off to find his friends to come and eat with him. Of course none of this grain ever grew.

The seeds on the thin soil started to grow at once. The heat of the sun was reflected by the stone beneath. This grain grew beautifully, because plants like to be warm. But while plants like being warm, they object to being toasted. After these seeds got their start there came a very hot day. The sun blazed and blazed until the wheat plants felt as though they were living next to a big bonfire. The little roots tried to get away from the heat of the sun, down in the cool earth, but there was hard rock down there. They could not find moisture anywhere. So the wheat began to wither as if it had sun stroke. At last it shriveled up and died. So that seed did not amount to anything.

Meanwhile, in the bramble patch the wheat was growing. The thorns and thistles were growing along with it. All plants have to have enough to eat and drink, but thorns and thistles are like greedy children who try to get all the food and coke there is on the table. The thistles crowded out the wheat, and it died from lack of proper food and water. Nobody ever harvested any wheat from that corner of the field.

In the good ploughed land the man came back with a hoe, cut away all the weeds, and gave the wheat room to grow. Finally, the wheat came to harvest. These plants had grown good wheat, a hundred times as much as he had planted.

Later, someone asked Jesus what he meant by the story of the sower. Jesus said the seed is like the word of God, that is, like the message that comes to us from God in a sermon, or in a book. Some people have hearts as hard as the beaten path, so the word of God cannot grow in these hearts. Other people have hearts like the shallow soil. At first they are very interested in what they hear. They get full of joy and enthusiasm, and are determined to do great things. But they go home and someone teases them. Someone else tempts them—asks them to do something they know they should not do. All their good resolutions wither away, like the grain in the thin soil. Still other people have hearts like the bramble patch. The word of God starts to grow in their hearts and even does well for a while. But bad things that used to grow in their hearts begin to grow again: the thistles of lies, the briars of laziness, the brambles of selfishness. The good in their hearts is crowded out, and the word of God dries up and dies within them.

The easiest garden to take care of is a weed garden. It needs no care at all. But it is good for nothing. Jesus said that some people have weed gardens in their hearts. True citizens of the kingdom of heaven try every day to do the will of God. They ask Him to help them cut away the thistles, briars, and brambles inside them, and to make what is right grow strong. They are like the good ploughed land. With them God is well pleased.

17. TWELVE BASKETS OF LEFTOVERS

At this point in his work, Jesus sent his apostles out into the country two by two. He told them to go in different directions and to teach and preach as they had heard him do, and to cast out devils and heal the sick. They walked down pleasant roads by green fields, two along this road and two along that road, each man with a walking staff in his hand. They spoke in the market places and, if any good citizen invited them, they went home with that man to dinner and a good night's sleep. If they received no invitation, they slept on mounds of hay in the fields, and drank from cool mountain streams to quench their thirst.

Then came the time for them all to get together again, and to tell Jesus how God had blessed them beyond their expectations. Jesus saw that they were very tired. There had been so many people coming and going about them that they had little leisure or time to eat. So he asked them to go with him to a quiet place to rest. He knew that tired people cannot be of much use to their neighbors.

They all got into a boat and rowed across the lake, going ashore where there were no houses. There was a lot of grass there, and back away from the shore were low wooded hills. There they sat down to rest, talk, and compare their experiences. But the people had seen them departing, and they decided they also would go and join Jesus on the other side of the lake. As they walked around to the other side they passed through the villages and told others where they were going, inviting them to go along. Everywhere they went, the crowd increased. As they walked through the villages, the windows would be thrown open and people would say, "Where are you going? What is the matter?" The crowd would reply, "We are going around the lake to find the prophet of Nazareth." There came back the reply, "We will go with you." Wherever there was sickness in a home they would bundle up the sick and carry them along in the hope that the famed healing power of Jesus would help them also.

Jesus and his apostles were resting. After some time they heard a distant sound. One of them said, "It is like the sound of many voices." Another said, "I hear the tramping of many feet." They all looked up, and there was a large crowd coming toward them. They had time to prepare for the crowd, and when the people arrived, Jesus and his disciples spent much time in teaching and healing.

When evening arrived, the disciples came to Jesus and said, "This is a deserted place, and the time for the evening meal is long passed. Why don't you speak to the crowd and ask them to go away into the villages to find food, because they have nothing to eat?" Jesus said to Philip, "Where can we find food so these people can eat?" Philip answered, "It would take three hundred dollars to buy enough bread to give each one of these people just one piece." Jesus asked his disciples to go and find out how much food there was in the crowd. Andrew came back and said, "There is a boy here with five loaves of barley bread and two small fish. They could not possibly feed all these people." Andrew had forgotten that Jesus was a man who liked to take small things and make them great, to work from a small beginning to a great finish.

Jesus said, "Ask the people to sit down." They sat down in companies of one hundred and fifty each, and the total count came to about five thousand. Jesus took the five loaves and two fish and looked up to heaven and blessed them. Then he broke them up and divided the pieces among the disciples. They went out into the crowd and passed out the food. Their baskets seemed never to get empty, and there was enough food for everyone—the crowd had all it could eat. After they had finished eating, Jesus told the disciples to go around and gather up the left-overs, so nothing would be lost. When everything was gathered together, it filled twelve baskets with the bits and pieces from five loaves and two fish.

When the crowd saw the miracle Jesus had performed they said, "This is a true prophet that has come into the world." Others said, "He is the Messiah. Let us make him our king." Everyone rose up, and all five thousand shouted and waved their arms, calling him their king. Jesus wanted to go away, but they stopped him and tried to compel him to become their king. He told them he could never become that kind of king; he wanted to be the king of their hearts, not the king of their country. So he asked the disciples to go back across the lake, and sent the crowd home. Then he went up alone into the low hills to pray just as the sun went down.

That was the turning point in the ministry of Jesus. Up to that time his followers had been many, and crowds had greeted him and followed him wherever he went. There had been those who had disliked him and had even threatened to kill him, but the common people had been eager to hear him. Now there was a reaction. He had told them plainly and bluntly he would never become a king such as they wanted their Messiah to be. The people would not accept him as king of their hearts alone. From then on, many of his followers went back home and walked with him no more. He was not even sure of the twelve disciples, and said, "Will you also go away?" But Peter answered for them all and said, "Lord, to whom would we go? You have the words of eternal life."

Representatives from the Temple in Jerusalem called the next day. These scribes met Jesus as he walked in the streets of Capernaum. They scolded him in the presence of the people, saying that God was dishonored because he did not keep the customs. But Jesus scolded them back, telling them they dishonored God with their customs. He said their religion was on their lips, and not in their hearts. God did not care for their petty rules. He must be served by honesty, mercy, truth and a good life. Jesus called these scribes blind leaders of the blind.

From then on, in Galilee as well as in Judea, Jesus was hated by more and more people, and it was unsafe for him to be in his own country.

18. THE GOOD SAMARITAN

East of the river Jordan lies a land called Perea, which means the land beyond. It was there that Jesus spent the greater part of the last months of his life. He went into Jerusalem now and then, but he never spent the night there. It was too dangerous for him, as the priests and the Pharisees were seeking to have him killed for breaking the customs. In those days the customs were also the law.

Jesus had new followers gathered about him. One day he chose seventy of them and sent them out into the cities of Perea, just as he had sent out the Twelve throughout Galilee. So the Seventy went out, healing the sick, and preaching the kingdom of heaven. The people listened, especially the common and the poor people. The Pharisees despised the Seventy, but the men and women who lived on the farms, and the poor people who lived on the back streets of the towns, received them and listened to them. Many of the wise and the prudent also hated these followers of Jesus, just as they did in Judea. They thought they had all the knowledge and were very unhappy when someone came, teaching things they had never taught. It hurt their pride.

Once, when Jesus was teaching, a lawyer stood up and said, "Master, what shall I do to inherit eternal life?" This meant he wanted to know how to live forever. He asked this, not because he felt he was in danger of missing eternal life, or because he wanted Jesus to help him. He asked as a lawyer whose business it is to ask questions. Jesus answered, "You have your law books; what do you read there?"

In those days the law meant more than it does today. Nobody would think of looking into a modern law book to find out how to live forever. Our books are about contracts and mortgages, corporations and crimes. People read them to see how to keep out of jail. But this lawyer's books were full of religion. They showed how good and bad actions affect not only the present, but the future life of men. The lawyer answered, "Thou shalt love the Lord thy God with all thy heart, and with all thy soul, and with all thy strength, and with all thy mind; and thy neighbor as thyself." Jesus replied, "That's right. Do this and you will live forever." But the lawyer was not satisfied and he asked, "Who is my neighbor?" You will remember that this was one of the chief differences between the teachings of Jesus and of the Jewish leaders. They felt that the Jews had no neighbors except those who were of their own race and religion. They did not feel that the Samaritans, or Gentiles, or even tax collectors, or sinners of their own race, were neighbors. They called them strangers and had no love for them whatever. Jesus replied in a parable, telling this story:

There was a man walking along a very lonely road, on his way from Jerusalem to Jericho. There were steep rocks on both sides, and the road had many sharp turns. Sometimes, the road was so deep among the cliffs that it was almost dark. Sometimes, it climbed so high on the hills that the traveler could look out for miles and miles. The man was not enjoying the journey. Every once in a while he stopped and listened. When he came to a corner he looked to see if there was anybody on the other side. The traveler was afraid of robbers.

The road was called the Red Road, partly because the rocks alongside had red streaks running through them, and partly because other red streaks on the ground were made from the blood of wounded men. Almost every day robbers would rush down upon a traveler and take away all he had, leaving him wounded and bleeding on the road. That is why this traveler was keeping such a sharp lookout as he hurried along.

In spite of all his looking and listening, a band of robbers came down from behind a rock. They caught the poor man, choked him, threw him down and beat him. After taking everything he had, they went away, leaving him lying in the road half dead and bleeding so as to make the Red Road redder than ever.

Soon a priest came along, also on his way to Jericho. He saw this poor man, but did not stop to help him. He crossed over to the other side of the road and went along without looking back. He was thinking only of himself and his own safety, hurrying ahead lest the robbers see him also.

Then along came another traveler. This man was a Levite, that is, he sang in the choir in the Temple in Jerusalem. He saw at once that something had happened, and he felt just as so many people feel when they see an accident. They want to see the victim and how he looks. Instead of going by on the other side of the road, he went and stood beside the wounded man. The poor man, groaning with pain, looked up and saw the Levite and said to himself, "Ah! Here is a friend who will give me some help. He has come to take me to a doctor." Do you know what the choir singer did? He turned away and left him.

This was as if a bunch of people were left on a desert island, looking every day for a ship. One day someone yells, "A ship! A ship!" and sure enough, there is a big ship coming directly toward them. So they yell to the ship and the captain hears them and waves back. Then suddenly, without a word of explanation, the captain turns the ship away and sails off, leaving them all behind. How bitter they all would be. It would have been better not to have seen the ship at all. This was the feeling of the wounded man as he watched the Levite turn around and leave him, climbing up the hill and disappearing from sight. Some time later the Levite would be singing in the Temple, and the priest praying in the Temple, just as if they thought that God sees only what happens in church, and does not know what happens on the highway.

At last there came along a man whom the priests and the Levites disliked, because he did not go to their church. This man was a Samaritan. He stopped and saw the wounded traveler and felt sorry for him. He stooped down and bound up his wounds, pouring oil and wine on the cuts. He lifted the traveler up on his own donkey and walked ahead, leading the animal. Soon they came to an inn, and the Samaritan got a place for the man to sleep, and sat with him all night, caring for him. In the morning he had to go about his business, so he called the landlord and paid the poor man's bill and gave the landlord some extra money to help pay for the traveler, saying, "Take care of him, and if it costs more, let me know when I come the next time, and I will pay the extra expense." The Samaritan was a stranger to the traveler. He knew that the man's friends and probably the man himself disliked Samaritans. Yet he did all this.

"Now," said Jesus to the questioning lawyer, "which of these men do you think was the neighbor to the traveler that was robbed by the thieves?" The lawyer answered, "The Samaritan that showed mercy on him." "Then," Jesus said to him, "go, and do likewise."

19. THE PRODIGAL SON

One of the reasons why Jesus was hated was that he was so kind to those whom the great and the rich people, and even the priests and ministers, disliked. They felt that the Gentiles, Samaritans, tax collectors and sinners should be avoided. Jesus felt that good people should not keep away from those who were wrong, different, or sinful. He said it was like asking doctors to keep away from the sick. For this reason Jesus spent a lot of time with those who were shunned by his fellow Jews. He felt both the ministers and priests were mistaken about God. He reminded them that a shepherd who has one hundred sheep will go searching for just one lost sheep, spending hours and hours looking through briars and brambles. When he finds the lost sheep he is so glad he brings in all his friends and neighbors to help him celebrate. Then Jesus told the parable of the prodigal son. It went like this:

Once upon a time there was a man who had two sons. The older son was quiet and reliable, but the younger son was restless and got tired of staying at home all the time. He wanted to go out and see the world. One day the younger son went to his father and asked for the share he was to receive when he became twenty-one years old. The father, being a fairly rich man, agreed to do this and divided his property between his sons.

The younger son immediately sold his share, took all his money, and went a long way off into the wide world. He had a fine time. He spent his money as if it was going out of style. He bought what was sweet to eat and sour to drink, thinking of nothing except how to have an even better time tomorrow. The sweets he ate made him fat and lazy, the sour drinks he had gave him a headache, and none of his pleasures lasted for very long at a time. But he thought he was enjoying life at its best. One morning he woke up to find he had no money left. Everything his father had given to him was gone. Soon he found that at the same time he had lost all his money, he had also lost all his fine friends. There were many young men and young women who had used him to receive gifts and favors while he had money, but now they no longer wanted to bother with him. Of course, he had not ever been a true friend to them. He had not cared about anyone but himself. He had never helped anyone, so now nobody helped him.

There was nothing he could do to keep from starving except to go to work. Work was hard to find. He had never had any real training, and any good paying job is skilled labor. He had to take an unskilled job and, of course, such work paid the smallest wages. The only job he could find was to be a swineherd, that is, to tend pigs. For a Jew, this was the most terrible job imaginable. Jews are taught not to eat pork, or touch a pig or its meat in any way. Here he was, tending them and living with them. He even had to eat the same food that was fed to the swine.

A few weeks of this life, and it was now natural that he should start thinking of his former home. He could shut his eyes and see how it all looked: the house in which he was born, with the trees all about it. There were rooms inside with nice furniture. In the dining room was a table and chairs, and his father, mother, and older brother were sitting there, having good Jewish food. Even his father's servants had enough to eat, and here he was starving, eating what little he had with the pigs.

He could stand it no longer. He said to himself, "I will go home. I will say to my father, 'I have sinned against heaven and against you. I am no longer worthy of being called your son. Please make me one of your hired servants!' " He quit his job as a swineherd and started home.

The day he approached his home his father was out looking down the road. Way down the street, walking slowly like a tired man after a long trip, came a man. His clothes were ragged and dirty, and he looked like a tramp, yet he had a familiar look.

So the father looked again, and sure enough, it was his younger son.

What did the father do? Did he say: "There comes my bad son who has disgraced himself and his family. He has spent all his money and is coming back for more. He thinks I will forgive him, but he is very much mistaken."? Or did he say, "Yes, that is my son. Now what shall I do? Shall I take him back or not?" No, he ran toward his son and met him way down the road. He had compassion and greeted him; he put his arms around him and kissed him. The son began to say the words he had planned, "Father, I have sinned against heaven and you, and am no longer worthy to be called your son." His father called him into the house and ordered his servant to bring his best robe and put it on his son, and to place a ring on his finger. Then he ordered another servant to go out and kill the fatted calf, the one they had been saving for the celebration of New Year's Day. He told the servant, "Kill it, and we will eat and be merry." So the servants cooked the very best dinner they knew how to prepare. The neighbors were called in, and after dinner men were brought in with musical instruments, and everybody began to dance.

There was one exception to all this celebrating. The older brother was out in the field working, and did not know his brother had returned. When he came home for supper he was quite surprised to hear all the noise of laughing, music, and dancing. All the young men and women in the area seemed to be there, having a wonderful time. The brother thought it strange there should be a party in his own home, and he had not been invited. He asked one of the servants what was going on. The servant told him his brother had come home, and his father had ordered the fatted calf to be killed and a party to be given in celebration. The older brother was angry and would not go in. "My brother has been a wicked fool," he said to himself. "Now he comes home and my father takes him in and makes a fuss over him. My brother should have a whipping instead of being given supper."

The father left the party and came out to talk to the older son. The son would not listen, replying to him, "Look, for many years I have stayed at home and minded your business, working early and late and never doing anything wrong. You have never given a party for me." His father replied, "Son, you are always with me, and all I have is yours. It is right that we should celebrate, because your brother was dead to us and now he is alive again. He was lost, and now he is found."

In this story Jesus meant that the Gentiles, Samaritans, tax collectors and sinners were like the prodigal son. The ministers and the priests were like the older brother. God is like the compassionate, loving, and forgiving father.

20. PALMS AND PSALMS

Jesus now felt that his mission in life was near the end. It was time for him to start on his last visit to Jerusalem. He knew he was headed toward his death on the cross. His Bible had foretold this in terms that could not be mistaken. It was again time for the Feast of the Passover, and the pilgrims from Galilee were on the road leading to Jerusalem. With the pilgrims came Jesus and the Twelve, out of the gates of Jericho and up the Red Road. At noon they rested beside the great rocks, and by night they had come to Bethany. The town was already full of travelers. Some slept in tents, some in the fields, and some in the homes of their friends. Jesus stayed with his friend Lazarus, but another friend named Simon prepared the evening meal for the company. It was there that Mary, mother of James and John, broke open an alabaster jar of precious ointment and poured it over the head of Jesus.

Some of the guests did not like that. One said, "Why was this ointment not sold for three hundred dollars, and the money given to the poor?" The speaker had another and worse reason for saying what he did. He was the treasurer of the Twelve. All their money was kept in one bag, and he carried the bag. It was never heavy. Not only was little put into it, but much was taken out to help the sick and the poor. Some of the Twelve were beginning to get suspicious that the treasurer was taking some of the money out of the bag and putting it into his own pocket. The treasurer's name was Judas Iscariot. Jesus replied to his comment by saying that Mary had done the right thing, and added, "She has anointed me for my burial."

Sunday arrived. That morning in Jerusalem the people were saying to each other in the Temple: "Will the Prophet come? Will he come to the Feast?" Some answered, "No, the priests and ministers are plotting to kill him. He will keep out of their reach." Others answered, "Yes, he has come already. He slept in Bethany last night, and today he will be in the city." On hearing that, many said, "Is he indeed coming? Let's go out to meet him." With this, many started out from Jerusalem, singing as they went, and waving branches of palm trees.

In the meantime Jesus was making his preparations in Bethany. Many years before, the writers of his Bible had written that the Messiah would come riding into Jerusalem, sitting on the colt of a donkey. In that country, horses were used for war, and donkeys were used in peace. Jesus sent two disciples into the next village, where a man lived that he knew. "There, at the corner of the street, you will find a colt tied to the door. Untie him and bring him to me." They went and found the colt, just as he had said. As they were untying the colt, the owner looked out and said to them, "What are you doing with my colt?" They replied, "The Master needs him." The owner then knew they had come from his friend, the prophet of Nazareth, as had been arranged.

They brought the colt and threw their robes over its back and seated Jesus on it. Off they started for the city. There was a large crowd following, and soon they met the crowd coming out of Jerusalem to meet him. After the two crowds had joined forces, they started to tear down branches from the trees, and waved them as Jesus rode by. Then they sang psalms: "Hosanna, blessed is he that cometh in the name of the Lord. Hosanna in the highest." The whole crowd rejoiced with great joy and praised God for all the wonderful works they had seen. This is the way they went, with laughing and singing, crying and shouting. One of the Pharisees said, "This is just too much. Jesus, scold your followers." Jesus answered, "I tell you that if I were to quiet these people, the stones alongside the road would start crying out."

In this way Jesus entered the city of Jerusalem. He had no crown on his head and no robe on his shoulders. He looked very different from other kings. Nevertheless, he came as a king to see whether his people would receive him, at last, or reject him. In spite of the procession along the road, as soon as they all entered the city, the crowd blended in with the general hubbub of traffic, and some of the people were no longer interested in him. Soon the rejoicing stopped and the singing faded away. Few people had any idea what the procession meant. Some of them were there from curiosity alone. They saw a crowd of farmers from Galilee, but city folks don't usually pay much attention to farmers from the country. Soon the men with the palm branches were lost in the general crowd which filled the streets.

The disowned king went into the Temple and looked around sadly and sternly. Then, with two of his disciples, he returned to Bethany to spend the night.

21. THREE DAYS OF THE HOLY WEEK

On Monday, Jesus came down the Mount of Olives, from Bethany, to go to Jerusalem. There he entered the Temple and looked again with sad and stern eyes at the scene he had observed the day before. You will remember that the Temple stood in a great big yard which was paved with stone, and which had a stone wall all around it. This yard was called the Court of the Gentiles, because the Gentiles—those who were not Jewish—were free to go into it as long as they did not pass through the gate of the Temple itself. When this Court was built, it was intended as a place where men who were not Jews could come in and pray.

Nobody was praying there that day. The Feast of the Passover, with its many pilgrims from out of town, had increased the number of sacrifices. Everyone visiting the holy city wanted to make a sacrifice on the altar of the Temple. Over the years the Court of the Gentiles had become a market place for the buying and selling of oxen, sheep, and doves that were to be offered as a sacrifice in the Temple. It had become more like a county fair than a church or temple. Not only were there stalls for the oxen and sheep, and cages for doves; there were also many tables at which money changers sat to trade small coins for big ones, or foreign money for Jewish money. Those buying or selling or trading money were shouting and yelling all over the Court, making prayer impossible.

This is what Jesus had seen the day before. Today he came back with a whip in his hand. Soon there was a great commotion in the place. Men and sheep and oxen were all rushing out the gate, and doves were flying all over the place. Behind them came Jesus with his whip. He turned over the tables of the money changers and the dove sellers, as he drove the people and animals before him, shouting, "Take these things out. Is it not written in the Bible, 'My house shall be called a house of prayer for all nations?' You have made it a den of thieves." There he stood, scolding the priests and the traders, in the name of God. In this way, for the second time, Jesus stood as a leader of the people. This time many were impressed, and a bunch of choir boys coming out of the temple started singing the same psalms that were sung the day before, "Hosanna to the Son of David."

On Tuesday, Jesus returned to Jerusalem and the Temple; the chief priests and the elders came up to him and said, "By what authority do you do these things? Who gave you this authority?" Still, they did not dare to take him prisoner or harm him in any way. There were too many pilgrims milling around who were on his side, believing him to be a prophet. All that day Jesus taught in the Temple. The Pharisees and the Sadducees argued with him, asking hard questions to try to mix him up, but he put them all to silence. He told them another parable.

At one time there were ten girls who were waiting and watching for a procession. They were the ten bridesmaids for a wedding. That night the bridegroom was to come and meet his bride so they could all go together to the wedding. It was dark and the ten had brought their lamps with them. The lamps were round bowls to hold oil, each with a wick floating in it. The bridegroom was late in coming and finally the bridesmaids fell asleep. At midnight there was a voice shouting "Behold, the bridegroom comes. Go out to meet him." The ten girls began to hurry to prepare their lamps. Five of them discovered that they had no oil in their lamps, so they would not burn. These foolish girls, who had neglected to fill their lamps ahead of time, tried to get the other five to share their oil with them. But the wise five had only enough oil for themselves and not a drop to spare. "You must go and buy some oil. If we give you any of ours, our lamps will go out too soon, and there will be no light to greet the bridegroom."

The foolish bridesmaids hurried away to find

some oil. Of course it was the middle of the night, and no stores were open. They ran from door to door trying to beg or borrow some oil, but nobody would help them. People were only angry to have been awakened at that hour of the night.

While the foolish five were scurrying around, the bridegroom came. The wedding procession with its music, lights, laughter and singing went past, and the wise five took their places in the procession, their lamps shining brightly. When all were in the house of the wedding, they shut and locked the door. Some time later the foolish five came to the door. They still had no oil for their lamps, but they stood in the darkness and knocked on the door. They called, "Lord, Lord, open to us." The bridegroom answered, "I don't know you. All my friends are here beside me in the house. Who are you that come so late?

When he had finished the story, Jesus said to the priests, "You had better stay awake and watch. You don't know the hour or the day when the Son of Man will come." Of course, we know that a lamp is of no use unless it has oil in it. A lamp without oil is like all good intentions—they alone won't get us anywhere. What Jesus meant was that we must prepare ourselves every day to live the kind of life he would want us to lead. Then our lives will shine as brightly as the oil lamps of the wise girls.

On Wednesday, the fear and the anger of the chief priests and the scribes, as well as of the elders of the people, came to such a fury that they held a meeting in the palace of the high priest, Caiaphas. They discussed how they could take Jesus and kill him. They decided they had to wait till the Feast was over and the pilgrims had gone home. They did not dare to do it with the pilgrims still around. While they were discussing this, there was a knock on the door, and someone came with strange news. "There is a man here who says he is one of the disciples of the prophet. Shall we let him in?" "Yes, admit him," they said. In came one of the Twelve, the troubled Judas Iscariot. He said, "What will you give me if I deliver Jesus to you? I can lead you to a place where you can grab him quietly and take him away without any trouble from the crowds. What will you pay me?" They promised to pay him thirty pieces of silver. So he went out of the meeting of the clergy, leaving them very glad with the turn of events.

22. THE LAST SUPPER

On Thursday, the Feast of the Passover began. You will remember that God had told the Jewish people ages ago always to remember the day they were set free.

When the anniversary came around, century after century, the Jews celebrated by sitting down to the same kind of supper. This was to make them remember how God had delivered them out of Egyptian slavery. They still do this every year, even now.

Jerusalem was full of people, for the lamb must be offered for sacrifice in the Temple, and the meal must be eaten in the holy city. Every house was full of guests. In every market the men were buying lambs, and in every kitchen the women were getting ready to cook the lambs. That morning the disciples asked Jesus, "Where do we go to eat the Passover?" Judas stood in the group, listening. To-

127

day, for the first time this week Jesus would stay in the city after dark. Where would he stay? Where could he send the priests to capture Jesus? It would be a perfect setup. All the people would be in their homes, sitting at their Passover supper, and Jesus could be arrested without any noise or interference.

Jesus saw the face of Judas. A man with such thoughts in his heart could not help but show them in his eyes. Jesus had seen Judas change in the last few weeks, ever since he had told the disciples he would be put to death. Judas had continued with the Twelve, but he was not at ease with them. He had hoped, as all of them had hoped, that Jesus would appear in Jerusalem with the power of a king. During the procession of the Palms, Judas had held his head up high with hope, but the procession ended as a failure for Judas, and his hopes vanished into thin air. Then on Monday, when Jesus had driven the traders out of the Temple, Judas knew the Sadducees would never forget that, so he felt it was all over. Jesus knew that Judas had lost hope, and with it he had lost faith.

Judas listened eagerly to find out where the supper would be eaten, but Jesus was able to give directions without telling the exact spot. Turning to two disciples he knew he could trust, he said, "Go into Jerusalem. As you pass the gate you will see a man in the street carrying a pitcher of water. Follow that man. When he goes into a house, go after him and ask for the master of the house. Tell him, 'The Master sends you this message: Where is the guest chamber, where I shall eat the Passover with my disciples?' He will show you a large upper room; make ready to have the Feast supper there." Of course Judas could not know where to direct the priests.

The two men went and found everything just as Jesus had predicted. There was a large upper room, reached by outside stairs. In it was a table with couches placed around it. Peter and John first took the lamb to the Temple for the sacrifice, and then brought it back to have it cooked. All things were ready for the supper. The sun set, and darkness came. Under the cover of the darkness, Jesus and the other disciples made their way down the Mount of Olives, into the city and to the upper room.

The disciples started to argue as to which of them would sit next to Jesus. Deep down inside they felt that whoever could sit next to him would be considered the greatest of the Twelve. Jesus read their thoughts and did not like them; he decided to teach them a lesson. He got up from the table, took off his robe, and took a towel. Then he poured water in a basin and began to wash the disciples' feet and wipe them with the towel. In that country men wore sandals. It was the custom for a servant to wash the feet of guests who came in from the heat and dusty roads. Jesus was taking the part of a servant. Peter spoke for them all, and said, "Lord, you wash my feet? Never will you wash my feet!" But Jesus insisted and washed the feet of them all, even Judas. Then he put his robe back on again and took his seat at the table. "Do you know what I have done? I, whom all of you call the greatest, have washed your feet like a servant. That is what the greatest ought to do. He only is truly great who is serving others."

The Passover supper was eaten. After the meal was finished there came a solemn end of the Feast. A cup of wine was blessed and passed, each person dipping herbs in the cup and eating them. Here Jesus stopped and looked about the table and said, "I tell you now that one of you will betray me. The writings in the Bible must be fulfilled where it is written. 'He that eateth bread with me hath lifted up his heel against me.'" They were all very sad and started asking Jesus, "Is it I?" Finally, Judas asked in a faint voice, "Is it I?" And Jesus replied to him, "What you do, do quickly." He said it in such a way that no one knew the meaning of it. Some thought that Jesus was only sending the treasurer out on some errand. Of course, Judas knew what he meant. He got up from the table and left them, going to seek the priests.

Then came the blessing of a second cup, and the singing of psalms. As he blessed this cup he passed it to his disciples, telling them to share it, saying, "I will not drink any more until I drink in the Kingdom of God." With this, they began to understand that the end was near and this was their last supper together.

Then Jesus took the bread and broke it, giving pieces to each disciple, and saying, "Take, eat: this is my body, which is given for you; do this in remembrance of me." Then came the cup with which the Passover supper ended. When he gave thanks, he gave it to them, saying, "This is my blood of the new testament, which is shed for you and for many, for the remission of sins; do this as oft as ye drink it, in remembrance of me." He told them he was to die, but now he told them he was to die for them and for many. He asked them to remember.

"I see you are very sorry," he said. "Sorrow has filled your hearts. The time has come, yes, the hour is now here, when you will be scattered and will leave me alone. I will give you peace. Be of good cheer. I have overcome the world." Then he prayed with them, and they sang some more psalms. The supper ended, and they all went back to the Mount of Olives.

23. THE GARDEN OF GETHSEMANE

The full moon was shining as Jesus and the eleven disciples came down the outer stairs from the upper room. The streets were still, except for sounds of merry voices coming from the houses where happy people sat at their Passover supper. They met no one on the way and passed through the gate of the city without any trouble. The road ran downhill into a deep valley, then crossed the bridge of a little stream called the Kidron. At the foot of the Mount of Olives was a little garden of olive trees, called Gethsemane.

On the way, the disciples had continued the discussions they had started in the upper room. Finally Jesus said to them, "The time has now come—the time I have been telling you about. The Pharisees and the Sadducees will arrest me and bind me. They will mock me and spit on me and kill me. You are my dear friends who have stayed beside me, even when all others have deserted me. Now you too will desert me." Peter spoke up and said, "I will never offend you, nor will I be offended by you." Jesus replied, "I tell you, Peter, that tonight, before tomorrow morning dawns and the cock crows twice, you will deny me three times." Peter replied, "I am ready to go with you both into prison and to death. Even if I should die with you, I will not deny you in any manner."

When they came to the gate at Gethsemane, Jesus asked eight of the disciples to wait there while he took Peter, James, and John with him back into the deeper shadows of the trees to pray with him. Jesus began to be troubled. He saw more clearly than ever before the certainty of his death. He was not afraid. He could escape quite easily. All he had to do was to walk out of the garden, up the hill, past Bethany, and into the country or desert. No man would harm him. If he would live in peace and quietness, no Pharisee or Sadducee would touch him. All they wished for was that he be silent. He could stay alive if he returned to the bench of a carpenter. But that was completely impossible. He had come, the Son of God, in the name of God, to teach the truth of God. That was his whole life. He could not imagine going on living and not doing that.

He had come with such a mission but had been rejected. His love for every man seemed to be the reason he was so hated. He left the three disciples there and went a little further into the garden, where he fell on his knees and prayed, saying, "O my Father, let this cup pass from me. Nevertheless, not as I will, but Thy will be done."

Now there was a noise of hurrying feet on the road that led from the city. Torches were seen flickering through the trees by the bridge across the Kidron. Jesus knew what they meant. He said, "The time has come. I have been betrayed into the hands of sinners. Get up, let us go to meet them. The one that betrayed me is here."

Judas had gone from the last supper to find the men to whom he had sold his soul. They probably had gone to the upper room, only to find that they were too late there. Judas knew he would find Jesus and his disciples in the garden of Gethsemane. Many times they had spent the night there. Judas knew every tree and could find his way past every corner. Now he led the band of servants of the high priest, who carried lanterns, torches, and weapons. Judas had given them a signal, saying, "The one that I kiss will be Jesus. Take him and lead him away safely." As soon as he reached the little band he went right up to Jesus and kissed him, saying, "Master, Master."

The servants of the high priest took Jesus and bound his hands. Peter drew his sword, and cut off the ear of one of the servants. Another of the disciples also had a sword and began to draw it. But Jesus said, "Put up your sword. Do you not know that if I were to ask my Father, he would instantly send me an army of angels? But it must not be." When they heard that, all the apostles turned around and ran away through the trees of the garden, leaving Jesus all alone.

24. CHRIST BEFORE CAIAPHAS

It was now past midnight. The servants of the high priest led Jesus away from the garden of Gethsemane, across the Kidron bridge and up the hill to the city gate. When they entered the city the people seemed to be asleep. The streets were empty and all the windows were dark. Soon the sound of running feet was heard, along the pavement. The palace of the high priest was all lit up. Servants came running out of the front door, first down one street, and then down many others. They would stop in front of a large home and knock on the door. The owner of the house would look out and say, "What is the matter?" The servants would answer, "He has been arrested; you know who. There is to be a meeting of the Sanhedrin immediately, where he will be put on trial."

The Jewish people had two rulers. One was Pontius Pilate, the Roman governor, who was the head of state. The other was Caiaphas, the High Priest, who was the head of the church. The high priest could do nothing without the consent of the standing committee, called the Sanhedrin. These were the men called out of their beds to come to the trial. While Jesus was being led along in the middle of the police and a small crowd, they were putting on their clothes and going to the palace of the high priest. Finally Jesus was brought in and the trial began.

The high priest asked Jesus about his disciples and his doctrine. Jesus replied, "I always spoke openly to the world. I often taught in the synagogue and in the Temple, which is the way we Jews do our teaching. I have said nothing in secret. Why do you ask me? Ask those who heard me what I said to them. They all know what I said." As he finished, one of the servants of the high priest slapped him in the face and said, "Do you answer the high priest in that way?" Jesus turned calmly and said quietly, "If I have said anything evil, say so, but if I have spoken the truth, why do you hit me?" The high priest did not scold the servant for being brutal.

Now the priests and elders and all of the council tried to find false charges against Jesus, so they could put him to death. They were determined to kill him, but they wanted to do it legally. They knew that many people thought Jesus was a prophet. They were afraid they might be put on trial for what they were doing, so they were very careful to follow the law exactly. If they could not find any witnesses who could bring true charges against Jesus, they would find some who would bring false charges, that is, who would lie.

It seems that one day while Jesus had been teaching in the Temple, he had said something that no one understood very well. Whether the words were a mystery, or whether there was so much confusion that they were not heard very well, we do not know. Anyway, two witnesses now came forward to charge Jesus with claiming he would destroy the Temple of God, and then rebuild it in three days. But these two false witnesses could not agree on the exact words Jesus had used. Therefore these charges could not be a legal charge, so they needed other evidence against him.

The high priest, dressed in his robes of office, stood up in the middle of the meeting, and asked Jesus, "Have you nothing to say?" Jesus did not reply at all. The high priest then said, "I demand, by the living God, that you tell us whether you are the Christ, the Son of God?" This was the question that Jesus had been waiting to answer in full. Before this time he had not proclaimed that he was the Christ that was promised in the Jewish Bible. He had admitted this to the disciples when they had asked him, but he had told them not to tell anyone else. Now he stood looking into the faces of the leaders of the people and the heads of the church. "Yes," he said, "I am the Christ, and you shall see the Son of God sitting on the right hand of power, and coming in the clouds of heaven."

The high priest took the long flowing linen robe he was wearing and tore it from the top to the bottom. In those days this was the way men showed great excitement. "He has spoken blasphemy." he yelled. That means he accused Jesus of speaking against God. "He claims to be the Christ, the Messiah, that the prophets have promised will come to us. What further need do we have for witnesses? You have heard him speak against God. What do you think?" Of course they all had decided to vote against him long before he had made this declaration. This just clinched it for them. They all replied, "He is guilty enough to be put to death."

The church, however, did not have the power to put any man to death. That power belonged to the state. Caiaphas had condemned Jesus, but in order for him to be killed, he must be tried by Pilate. It was still too early in the morning to see Pilate, so Jesus was handed over to the servants to wait till Pilate could see him. The scribes and elders all returned home. Jesus, with his hands tied, stood with the servants. They decided to have some fun with him. They put a blindfold across his eyes. Then a servant would dance around him and hit him, first on one cheek and then on the other, saying, "If you are a prophet, prophesy now. Who was it that hit you?"

In the meantime, two of the disciples found that no one had been following them when they had run away, so they turned back. Keeping in the shadow of the walls and houses, they came up to the palace of the high priest. No one there seemed to be interested in anything but the trial, so they went in. It was cold in the early spring morning, and the servants had built a charcoal fire on the stone pavement and stood around warming themselves. Peter joined them, holding out his cold hands to the warm fire. It was quite plain by looking at Peter that he was from the country. Now, as he stood there talking with the others, it was also plain that he was from Galilee. His clothes hinted at it and his accent proved it. The fishermen of Galilee had a way of talking which the people of Jerusalem thought odd. The fishermen did not pronounce their words the same as the people of the city.

A maid-servant said at once as he started talking, "Are you not one of this man's disciples?" Peter, already tired from the lack of sleep, nervous and afraid, and now taken by surprise, said, "I am not." John and he had come to see the end—the end of all their hopes and dreams. There were no longer any disciples. That beautiful brotherhood had been broken up. Jesus was on trial for his life, and they would not see him any more. So Peter spoke out of the bitterness of his heart. He had been a disciple, but he was not any longer.

Peter continued to stand by the fire, trying to pick up any news as to what was going on. He looked so miserable that another maid-servant said to him, "You also were with Jesus of Nazareth." Peter replied, "I don't know what you are talking about." He went through the gate into the street. The first faint light of dawn began to streak across the sky and a rooster crowed in a barnyard close by. Peter started back, but as he turned, the woman called to the men at the fire, "See that man! Isn't he one of them?" "Yes," they replied. "He is a Galilean. His speech shows that." Another man said, "Yes, I saw him in Gethsemane with Jesus." Peter again replied, "I do not even know this man of whom you speak." Again the rooster in the barnyard could be heard.

At this moment Jesus was led through the passage and heard Peter say these words. Jesus turned and looked at Peter. Peter remembered that Jesus had said to him, "Before the cock crows twice, you will deny me three times." He went out into the street and cried bitterly.

25. CHRIST BEFORE PONTIUS PILATE

The dawn broke, and it was Friday. This is the same day we now call Good Friday. Early in the morning the servants of the Sanhedrin took Jesus to deliver him to Pontius Pilate.

The officers of the Sanhedrin went along, of course. They had to bring the charges against Jesus before Pilate. These officers already had been to their daily prayers while Jesus was being taken from the palace of the high priest to the palace of Pilate. They had prayed before the altar in a quiet way. These people who were so determined to kill Jesus were not bad men. They were quite sure they were doing the right thing. They said their prayers with a clear conscience. They acted as they did toward Jesus, not because their hearts were full of sin, but because their minds were full of prejudice. They considered themselves good churchmen.

Jesus was not considered a good churchman in their way of thinking. He wanted to upset the old ways of doing things. That was the real reason behind the whole matter. They were afraid that Jesus would do harm to their church.

There was an unpleasant interruption in the middle of this early church service. A man came racing into the Temple, waving his hands and yelling in a wild and excited voice, saying, "I have sinned. I have betrayed innocent blood." In he came, with the thirty pieces of silver in his hands, wanting to give them back. He had had a sleepless night. He had betrayed his friend, but there was still some good in him. Nobody knows why he did his deed. He himself did not know why he had done it. Now he came to make a desperate try to right a wrong he had done. "Let him go. He has done nothing wrong. I have betrayed innocent blood." "What is that to us?" said the priests and elders, frowning at him. Then Judas raised his hands and threw the thirty pieces of silver toward them. The coins flew all over the temple floor, rolling and ringing as they fell. The traitor Judas turned, ran out, and committed suicide by hanging himself.

The priests, scribes and elders now had Jesus outside the palace of Pilate. Pontius Pilate was a Roman and a heathen. When he thought of God, which may not have been very often, he thought of him as Jupiter. When he said prayers, which again may not have been very often, he sprinkled grains of incense on burning coals before an idol. The delegation stood outside the palace of Pilate, and called for him to come out on his balcony. Quite a crowd was gathering. The news had spread that Jesus had been arrested. Those who cared about Jesus were in hiding. This crowd was just curious. They did not care.

Pilate heard the crowd while he was eating his breakfast, and went out. "What charges do you bring against this man?" he asked. "We charge that he claims to be a king, King of the Jews." That was a serious charge. It was a charge of treason. Caesar at Rome was the King of the Jews. The scribes wanted Pilate to believe that Jesus was leading a revolt against the Roman authority. It was easy to believe. The Jews hated the Roman rule and had rebelled many times, sometimes for a day in a single city, and at other times in a fierce and wide revolt. At this very moment Pilate had in his prison a man named Barabbas, who had led a riot in the streets of Jerusalem.

Pilate did not believe this charge. He already knew something about Jesus. He was aware that the priests had arrested him because of envy. He knew that Jesus had not preached anything against Rome. His spies had reported that to him long ago. He had Jesus brought into the palace, leaving the crowd outside. He asked Jesus, "Are you the King of the Jews?" Jesus answered, "Why do you ask? Do you say this on your own, or did others accuse me of this?" Pilate replied, "Am I a Jew? Your own nation and chief priest have brought you here and charged you with this. What have you done?" Jesus said, "Yes, I am a king, but I am not a king of a nation on earth. In my kingdom there is neither a crown nor an army. I came into the world to preach the truth. The kingdom of God, which I preach, is the kingdom of truth." Pilate did not understand. "What is truth?" He asked. He did not expect an answer. It was plain there was no cause for him, the Roman governor, to interfere in this dispute within the Jewish church. He went back out on the balcony of the palace and said to the crowd, "I find no fault at all in this man."

The whole council of the Sanhedrin got very mad and also fearful. They had brought Jesus to Pilate and now Pilate was about to set him free. So they yelled out all kinds of charges against Jesus. One said, "He forbids the people to pay taxes." Another said, "He has set the whole land in an uproar, from Galilee to Judea." Pilate replied, "If he is a Galilean, he belongs to Herod." In this way Pilate tried to transfer the case to Herod, but he was not successful. The crowd grew in size, and became more vocal. He knew something had to be done.

Pilate thought of the man Barabbas. He said, "There is another man I have in jail who is charged with the same crime. He too has taken part in a rebellion. You have your choice. I will follow the old custom and release a political prisoner at your Passover. Which do you choose, Jesus or Barabbas?" The crowd yelled as if with one voice, "Barabbas!" Pilate said, "What do you want me to do with this man who calls himself the king of the Jews?" The crowd called out, "Crucify him!" Then Pilate said to them, "Why, what evil has he done?" They had no answer for that question, so they continued to yell, "Crucify him!" Another man in the crowd called out, "If you let this man go, you are no friend of Caesar. Whoever makes himself a king speaks against Caesar." That settled Pilate's mind. He did not dare be charged with allowing treason to go unpunished. So he called for a basin of water. Before the whole crowd he washed his hands, saying, "I am innocent of the blood of this fine person. It is you who have charged him." The crowd answered, "His blood be upon our heads and on our children." Pilate released Barabbas.

Jesus was then given over to the soldiers. They took him into a common hall and gathered about him. They took off his clothes and put on him a tattered old purple robe. They made a crown out of thorns and pushed it on his head. Then they pretended to salute him, bowing down on their knees in front of him, saying, "Hail, King of the Jews." Then they would slap him and spit in his face and laugh.

After all this, Pilate tried once more to release Jesus. He appealed to the pity of the crowd. Jesus was led out with his purple robe and thorny crown. Pilate said, "Look, I bring him out to you to show you that I find no fault in him. Look at him. Look at the man!" When the crowd saw Jesus, they had no pity in their hearts. They yelled out again, "Crucify him! Crucify him!" "What!", shouted Pilate, "Shall I crucify your king?" They all answered, "We have no King but Caesar." This was the last word. They put Jesus' own clothes back on him and he was led away to be crucified.

26. CRUCIFIED, DEAD AND BURIED

The death sentence was pronounced a little before nine o'clock in the morning. It was decided to proceed without delay, because of the still present pilgrims in the city, many from Galilee. Jesus was led out onto the road to the place of execution.

Pilate's soldiers marched in front of him and behind him. Two thieves had been brought out of jail to join in the procession, because they also were to be crucified. A crowd formed and followed—churchmen, pitying women, and curious onlookers with no feelings one way or the other. Well behind, came a few friends. The apostle John was with his mother. Also there were Mary Magdalene, another Mary, the mother of James, and a third Mary, who was the mother of Jesus.

Jesus and the two thieves had to carry their own crosses. One of the soldiers had a hammer and some big nails, or spikes, to use in the crucifixion. Another soldier carried a board with the letters printed on it, "King of the Jews". This was to be nailed over the head of Jesus on the cross to show the crime of which he was charged. The priests had begged Pilate to change this to read "I am the King of the Jews," to show it was a false claim he had made, but Pilate refused to change a word.

The cross was very heavy and Jesus was very tired. All night he had had no sleep. Since the last supper in the upper room he had received nothing to eat. He had had to say good-bye to his friends, submit to arrest, and stand trial twice, once before Caiaphas and once before Pilate. He had been forced to stand most of this time, and had been given several beatings. All this was just too much. He stumbled and fell in the street beside the city gate.

At this moment there was a man entering the gate who was broad and strongly built. His name was Simon of Cyrene. The soldiers stopped Simon and taking the cross off the shoulders of Jesus, put it on the shoulders of Simon. The procession then moved on, Simon carrying the cross for Jesus.

The women in the procession began to cry and wail when they saw that Jesus could not carry the cross. Jesus turned to them and said, "Daughters of Jerusalem, do not weep for me. Weep for yourselves and for your children. The city that crucifies the innocent will be punished." Many years later this did happen. The Romans set up hundreds of crosses along the same road, and on them they crucified the chief citizens of Jerusalem. At the same time they leveled the city to the ground so that not a stone or brick was left standing on top of another.

At last they came to a hill called Golgotha. The crosses were laid on the ground and holes were dug in the ground for the crosses to be put into in an upright position. Jesus and the two thieves were fastened to the crosses by having nails driven through their hands and feet. The crosses were tipped up and placed in the holes. Up till this time Jesus had not made a sound. He had not made a sound when they had pounded the nails through his hands and feet. Now, as he hung there on the cross, he started praying for the people who had done this to him, saying, "Father, forgive them, for they know not what they do."

It was the custom, during crucifixions, to give the victim an opiate, or drug, to deaden the pain. The soldiers soaked a sponge with a mixture of wine and myrrh, holding it up to Jesus on a long stick. He tasted it and knew what it was and refused to drink it. He would meet his death with a clear mind. At the foot of the cross the soldiers prepared to divide his clothes into four parts, one part for each soldier. It was the custom that the soldiers get the clothes from the victims. But Jesus' robe was all one piece of cloth without a seam. It was impossible for them to divide it. They said to each other, "Let's not tear it. Let's get some dice and throw the dice to see which one will get the whole robe." Then the soldiers, along with many in the crowd, began to call out to Jesus saying, "If you are the King of the Jews, save yourself." And the two thieves joined in, saying, "If you are the Christ, save yourself and us." But one of the thieves joined only faintly in this taunting of Jesus. Finally he scolded the other by saying, "Do you not fear God? This is the hour of death. We, at least, are guilty and are being justly punished, but this man has done nothing wrong." Then he turned to Jesus and said, "Lord, remember me when you come into your kingdom." Jesus replied, "Truly, I say to you, today you will be with me in paradise."

Then Jesus saw his mother standing by with the apostle John, whom he loved best of all. He said to his mother, "John is now your son." To John he said, "This is now your mother." From then on John took mother Mary into his own home.

The painful morning passed. At noon the clouds rolled up, hiding the sun, and it became very dark. Jesus cried from the cross, "My God, my God, why have you forgotten me?" This is the first sentence in a psalm that all the Jews knew by heart. It was written by a man who thought that God had deserted him, but then found out that God loved him through all his suffering. The Jewish word for "My God" is "Eloi". Some of the people in the crowd mistook the sound of the word when Jesus spoke it, thinking he had said "Elias." "Listen," they said, "He calls for Elijah. Let's see if Elijah will come and take him down." Even then, some thought a miracle might happen. They had visions of the sky opening up and a fiery chariot coming down, driven by Elijah, the prophet of old times. Then Jesus said, "I am thirsty." The soldiers filled a sponge full of vinegar and lifted it up to him on a long stick. Then he cried in a loud voice, "It is finished. Father, into Thy hands I commend my spirit." Then Jesus died.

It was three o'clock. The next day was the Sabbath. According to their custom the Sabbath started at sundown the previous day. The priests asked Pilate to have the two thieves killed to put them out of their misery so that all bodies could be removed before the holy day. Pilate gave his permission. The soldiers came and broke the legs of the two thieves and killed them, but they found that Jesus was already dead. Just to make sure, they stuck a spear in his side before they took him from the cross.

Two men of wealth and prominence now became bold enough to come forward to claim the body of Jesus. Now that he was dead and no longer a threat, it was safe to show interest in his body. Joseph of Arimathea went to Pilate and asked for the body of Jesus. Nicodemus brought myrrh and aloes to embalm it. They took the body and put it in a cave in Joseph's garden. Then, because it was so late in the day, they rolled a big stone in front of the cave so that no animal could get in. They left, expecting to come back later to finish with the embalming process. By the time the moon came up, there was no one there except a group of soldiers pacing up and down before the grave of the "King of the Jews."

27. THE EMPTY TOMB

The disciples of Jesus had one consolation. Nothing could rob them of the memory of their friend. All day Saturday they thought of him, and even though it was their Sabbath, they may not have gone to church that day. How could they worship in a temple with the Sadducees, or in a synagogue with the Pharisees, who had brought death to their master? Somewhere they met. Perhaps it was in the upper room so they would be able to remember that last supper together. Maybe they broke the bread and drank the wine, "in remembrance of Him."

These men had had an experience that nobody else had experienced since the world had begun. They had known a Perfect Man. It is true that the heads of the church did not think he was perfect. They had criticized him and found faults in him, and even wound up killing him. But what seemed like faults to them seemed like virtues to the disciples. Millions since then have agreed with the disciples. Jesus was the one Perfect Man. In him our human nature came to its highest excellence. He lived our human life and was tempted in all things as we are tempted, yet he did not sin. The best men who have lived since that time have tried to live like Jesus. None have succeeded.

Jesus, the Son of God, had died for us. Other men have died for us, some even for the love of God. For hundreds of years men have asked, "Does God care?"

Does it really matter whether we do right or wrong? Does God care? Does it matter to Him if we suffer sometimes for doing the right thing? Does He know this world is full of sin and pain? Does God care? There is no answer in this world of nature. The Son of God came down to tell us of the love of God. He told us that God cares for every one of us. He told us that God feels toward sinners as the father did about the prodigal son, and that every sinner who is truly sorry about his sins will be forgiven. Jesus showed this to us by his life and by his death. For our sake he died on the cross. "Greater love has no man than this; that he give up his life for his friends."

The fact that Jesus died for us to save us from our sins was not all. In Jesus was fulfilled the saying from the Bible, "God so loved the world that he gave his only-begotten son, that whosoever believeth in him should not die, but have everlasting life."

Even the disciples, who had been his closest friends could not quite understand that. They lay awake all Friday night and Saturday thinking about it. Then they got together and talked things over. They had seen him die. They had seen the wounds in his hands and feet and then, finally, the spear in his side. He was as dead as the two thieves. Where were all his great words now? Was this the end of all their thoughts and hopes?

Those were the men who had followed Jesus. The women were different. Like most women they were more compassionate and, perhaps, more practical. Two of them were the mothers of apostles: Salome, the mother of James and John, and Mary, the mother of James the Little. Then there were Mary Magdalene and Joanna, the wife of Herod's steward. These women knew that Joseph and Nicodemus had not finished with the embalming of the body. It had been wrapped in linen, and aloes and myrrh were on hand to finish the process. The next day had been the Sabbath, so no one had gone to the tomb to complete the embalming. On the first day of the week, it being Sunday, the women got together to go to the grave, in the garden where Jesus was buried.

As they came near the garden, one of them said, "The stone, the great big stone that Joseph and Nicodemus rolled in front of the cave, how can we roll it away?" When they came within sight of the grave, they saw that the stone had been rolled away. They did not know what to think. They came up to the opening and looked in. The grave was empty. They said to each other, "They have taken away our Lord." Who could have taken the body, or where they could have taken it, nobody could imagine. The tomb was empty, that was plain. As they turned to go, they saw two men in white shining robes. The women were afraid and fell on the ground in front of these men. But the men said, "Why do you look for the living among the dead? He is risen. He is not here. Remember how he told you in Galilee, saying, 'The son of man must be given to sinful men and be crucified, and the third day rise again.'" Then they remembered those words. They had not understood. With this wonderful news the women hurried back to the city. They ran along the road in fear and joy, and great amazement.

When they came to the disciples they told them the tomb was empty. "The great stone is rolled away and the body is not there. We saw angels who told us that he who was dead is now alive." The apostles did not believe this. They did believe the women when they said the tomb was empty, but to think that Jesus had risen from the dead was beyond their belief. "You imagine it. There were no angels." They decided the women could have seen something else, so they decided to go see for themselves. Peter and John started for the garden together. John, the younger of the two, left Peter way behind and came to the garden first. The tomb certainly was empty. Nothing was there but the linen which had been wrapped around the body. There was no sign of violence or hurry. It did not look as if the grave had been robbed. Neither of them could decide what had happened. So they went back home, walking slowly, with their eyes on the ground, thinking and wondering.

28. JESUS REAPPEARS

It was still Sunday. All day the disciples were bothered with rumors. Somebody said that the women had seen not only an angel, but Jesus himself. He had met them, saying, "All Hail!" and they had come and touched him and worshipped him. Someone else said that there had been an earthquake during the night, and that an angel of God had come down and rolled away the great big stone from the mouth of the cave. The women had seen this angel, and his face was like lightning, and his clothes were white as snow.

Mary Magdalene reported that she had seen Jesus. She was standing by the door of the tomb, crying. She stooped down and looked into the cave, and there were two angels sitting on the ledge where the body of Jesus had lain. One of the angels said to Mary, "Why do you cry?" Mary answered,

"Because they have taken away my Lord, and I do not know where they have taken him." When she turned around she saw Jesus standing there, but she did not recognize him at first. Jesus said, "Why are you crying? For whom are you looking?" Mary thought it was the gardener, as her eyes were full of tears and she could not see very well. "Sir," she said, as if talking to the gardener, "If you have carried him away, tell me where you have put him and I will take him away." Jesus said, "Mary." Then she recognized him and cried, "My master!" Jesus told her not to touch him, but to go and tell the disciples. She went back to them, running all the way, telling them, "He is alive. I have seen him with my own eyes." Even then they would not believe.

That afternoon two men, one named Cleopas, took a long walk. They lived in a small village called Emmaus, about six miles out of Jerusalem. They had been in the city over the Sabbath and were returning home. They may have witnessed the crucifixion, or they may have spent the day with the disciples, we do not know. But we do know that they were friends and followers of Jesus while he lived. As they walked home, they discussed all the things that had happened that weekend. The dark cloud that had hung over the city, starting on Friday, had by now disappeared and the sun was shining again. It was a beautiful spring day. The flowers were in bloom all along the road and the birds were singing their hearts out in the gentle breeze. These two men did not see the sun. They did not hear the birds, or look at the flowers. As for the buds and blossoms, they could have been briars and brambles. The men would not have known the difference. Do you know what these two grown men were doing as they walked along? They were crying. Everyone they passed on the road noticed them. People stopped and looked back at them, saying, "I wonder what has happened? Have they had bad news? Maybe they are coming back from a funeral."

At last these two men came to the open country. The city was out of sight behind them. One of the men passing them on the road stopped and spoke to them. "As you walk along, you look so sad. What are you talking about, you two?" Cleopas answered, "You must be a stranger in Jerusalem or you would not ask. Don't you know the things that have happened these last three days?" The man said, "What things?" Cleopas answered, "The things about Jesus of Nazareth. He was a prophet and did wonderful things for people, preaching a new truth. Friday, the chief priest and Pilate condemned him to death and had him crucified. We believed in him with all of our hearts. We thought he was the Christ, the Messiah. Then this morning all kinds of things happened. The women of our band of believers went out to the tomb and found it empty. They came back saying that Jesus had risen from the dead. Some of our men went out to look, and they found that the tomb was empty, but they did not see anything else. The women had thought they saw some angels, but our men saw nothing, only an empty tomb. Some one had taken his body away. Do you wonder why we go home, crying?"

While Cleopas was saying this, the stranger was walking along beside the two men. He said to them, "Have you not read the Bible? Do you not know that Christ must suffer all these things? What is meant in the psalm where it is written, 'They pierced my hands and my feet?' What is meant in the chapter in Isaiah, where it is written, 'He is despised and rejected of men, a man of sorrows and acquainted with grief. He was wounded for our transgressions, he was bruised for our inquities. The chastisement of our peace was upon him, and with his stripes we are healed'?" The words he said and the tone of the voice in which he spoke, impressed the two men. "You thought," he said, "that Jesus could not be the Christ, the Son of God, because he died on the cross last Friday. Now you see that the holy men who wrote the Bible many years ago knew that the Christ must be put to death. It has all happened just as the prophets wrote it would happen. Christ dies, but he rises again from the dead." All this made their hearts turn from sadness to joy.

The two men came near their village, and the stranger turned as if to go a different way. They invited him to go with them to their house and stay for the night. When the time came for supper, they all sat down together, Cleopas, his friend, the women and children of the family, and the stranger. They asked the stranger to say the blessing. As he said it, he took the bread and broke it, giving a piece to everyone. Suddenly they knew him. It was Jesus himself. At that moment he vanished into thin air. He was no longer there.

Cleopas and his friend jumped up from the supper table and hurried back to Jerusalem, half running and half walking. There were no more tears in their eyes as they ran along the road.

That night the disciples were together, with the doors shut tight and locked. They were still afraid of the Pharisees and the Sadducees. Only ten of them were there. Judas was dead, and Thomas was so upset and sad that he stayed at home alone with his own thoughts and disappointment. The ten were sitting at the table, having just finished their supper. There was still some fish and some bread on the table that had not been eaten. Peter was talking excitedly. "I have seen him," he was saying. "He came and spoke to me. He is alive." There was a sound of running feet on the steps outside. There was a knock on the door and a voice said, "This is Cleopas of Emmaus with great news. Open up." They let him and his friend in, and they told the ten all about their meeting with Jesus. All of them then realized that he had risen indeed.

He had appeared to Peter, and now to the two men from Emmaus.

And as they were celebrating the good news, suddenly Jesus himself was standing in the middle of the group. The doors were shut and had stayed shut. He had not come in by those doors. He appeared, just as he had disappeared in Emmaus, suddenly, out of the thin air. He said, "Peace be unto you." But they were all afraid, thinking they had seen a spirit. He showed them his hands and his feet, with the marks of the nails on them. He took some fish and

some bread and ate it, so they could see it was really
Jesus and not just his spirit. Again he said, "Peace
be unto you. As my Father has sent me, so do I send
you." There he stood, in their sight. He was the
risen Lord. He who had died was now alive.

29. VISIONS OF JESUS

Jesus had now shown himself alive to most of the apostles and a few others. Ten of the apostles had seen him face to face. But there were two persons who would not believe, even on the word of those people they knew to be honest.

One of these unbelievers was James, the brother of Jesus. James had never believed that Jesus was the Son of God. Of course he believed that a king would come for the Jews. This was written in his Bible. But that his own brother with whom he had played as a child was the Christ seemed impossible for him to believe. At one time he had convinced himself and his other brothers that Jesus was out of his right mind, and together they had gone out to try to persuade him to come back to Nazareth. We are sure that all of his brothers loved Jesus, but none of them believed in him enough to become a disciple. Now that Jesus had come back to life, one of the first persons he sought out was his brother James. What he said, and what James answered, we do not know, but after that all of Jesus' brothers were constantly found in the company of the disciples.

The other unbeliever was Thomas. He seemed to have a gloomy way of looking at things. He had seen Jesus on the cross and could think of nothing but the nails in his hands and feet, and the gash in his side from the spear. The other disciples had told Thomas, "Last night at supper, while you were away, we saw Jesus. He came into the room where we were and blessed us." Thomas answered, "I know that all of you think so, but it is not something that I can believe unless I see it for myself. Unless I can see the prints of the nails in his hands, and put my fingers in those holes and in the gash in his side, I will not believe it." This went on for a week. The next Sunday came and the disciples were again in the upper room with the doors tightly shut. Again, Jesus appeared suddenly in the middle of the group, saying as before, "Peace be unto you." Then he turned to Thomas and said, "Stick out your finger and feel my hands, and then put your finger in the gash in my side so you can believe that I have risen from the dead." Thomas did as he was told and fell down on his face on the floor; he said, "My Lord and my God." Jesus said, "Thomas, because you have seen me, you have believed. Blessed are they that have not seen, and still believe." Because of this episode, down through the years Thomas has been known as "Doubting Thomas."

Sometimes even those who saw him did not believe. He was the same friend and teacher who had died on the cross. His body had the marks of the wounds from the crucifixion, but he was different in a mysterious way. Slowly the disciples realized he was quite different. He still had the same body. He demonstrated this by eating and drinking with them, and allowing them to touch him. But this body had changed too. It became usual for those meeting him not to recognize him at first. At other times they noticed that when he walked with them, the passers-by would see the disciples, but not Jesus. At times, only the disciples could see him. Yet, one time there was a gathering of over 500 people and Jesus appeared to all of them, and spoke with them. At last, there came a time when days and days would pass with no one seeing Jesus at all. Even on Sunday, which they had started to call "The Lord's Day," he did not visit with them. They did not know just what to think about this. One day Peter, Thomas, Nathaniel, James, John and two others, all fishermen, were talking together. Peter said, "I'm going to go fishing." The others all said, "We'll go with you." They could no longer be idle, wondering what would happen next. So they all got in a boat and fished all night, using a torch off the stern to attract the fish into their nets. They caught nothing. When dawn appeared the water changed from black to gray, and the thin line of land appeared.

On the shore someone stood on the beach and called, "Hey men, have you caught anything?" They called back, "No." He said, "Throw your nets out the other side of the boat." So they threw them out and caught so many fish they could not bring the net on board. Immediately John said, "It is the Lord." Peter, when he heard that, jumped into the water and swam ashore. The others rowed the boat in, dragging the net with the fish. As soon as they set foot on land, they saw a fire of coals burning, with fish on it. There was bread, and the stranger was standing by the fire. The stranger said, "Bring some of the fish you caught." Peter went to help, and they pulled the net on shore and counted the fish. There were one hundred and fifty-three nice big fish. The stranger then invited them to breakfast.

All this time they would look at the stranger and then back at each other. He seemed a very friendly stranger. They felt there was something familiar about him. They all knew in their hearts that it was Jesus, but he did not look like the Lord to them. They recognized him with their hearts rather than with their eyes.

Forty days went by like this. Some days were full of wonder and awe. Those were the days the Lord came and talked with the disciples. Other days were dull. These were the days they would expect the Lord to appear, but he did not come. They could not tell at what moment or at what place he might appear. Sometimes one man alone, going into the hills to pray, would suddenly find Jesus standing beside him. At other times he appeared to a crowd.

One reason that Jesus appeared to his followers was to make certain they knew that he had come back to life after his death on the cross. They saw him face to face and heard him speak. They knew beyond all doubt that he really was the Son of God.

Another purpose was to assure them that death is not the end. It just seems like the end. The body dies, and as far as we can see, the soul dies with it. What they needed was a voice from beyond the grave. They needed to have someone come back and tell them about it. Jesus came back and told them that death is not a wall, but a door. After we die, we shall live again.

Then he gave the disciples their last instructions. They were to go and teach what he had taught them. What they had heard in secret, they were now to declare openly. Those who heard the teaching and believed it, and desired to live in the new way, were to be baptized. This would initiate them into a new society. He had already told them how to break bread and eat it, and to pour the wine and to drink it in remembrance of him. This they were to do at the meetings of the new society.

One day, near Bethany, they asked Jesus a question that had long been in their hearts, but still remained unanswered. "Lord, will you now establish your kingdom in Israel?" He answered, "The kingdom is in your own hearts and in the hearts of those you will teach. You will be the founders of it. You will be my witnesses, telling how I came from heaven, the Son of God, to give all men life here and hereafter. Teach them to live as I have taught you, showing my spirit in your lives. And lo, I am with you always, even to the end of the world."

After these words were spoken he lifted his hands and blessed his disciples. While they watched, he was lifted up into the clouds and out of their sight. Jesus had been taken back to heaven. He was now to sit on the right hand of God the Father almighty, maker of heaven and earth.

Jesus still appears on earth. He appears in the heart of everyone who accepts him and his teaching. And the greatest part of his teaching is that everyone who believes in him will have everlasting life.